SIMON & SCHUSTER
Rockefeller Center
1230 Avenue of the Americas
New York, NY 10020

SIMON & SCHUSTER and colophon are registered trademarks
of Simon & Schuster, Inc.

For information about special discounts for bulk purchases,
please contact Simon & Schuster Special Sales:
1-800-456-6798 or business@simonandschuster.com

Designed by C. Linda Dingler

Manufactured in the United States of America

2   4   6   8   10   9   7   5   3   1

Library of Congress Cataloging-in-Publication Data is available.
ISBN 0-7432-4612-8

For My Darling Angels, Beatrice and Eugenie—
You are the blood in my veins,
the breath in my lungs,
the freckles on my face,
the joy in my heart.
You make my world complete
and have taught me how to live and how to love.
I love you both with all of my being.

CONTENTS

CONTENTS

CONTENTS

INTRODUCTION

Until recently, my changing age held no more signifi-cance to me than the barometric pressure or the gross na-tional product of Brazil. It was just a new number, an excuse for a nice dinner, and then I flipped the page to an-other year.

But as I turn forty-three, it seems to me an apt time for reflection, a time to share what I have learned, however slowly. For too long, my life was awash with inconsistency. I was like a river running in curves so broad that it never built any useful speed. I meandered through the uncon-sciousness of my youth and early twenties; the Sturm und Drang of my Buckingham Palace years; the perpetual crises of my thirties, when I first struck out on my own.

Now, at last, I have reached some perspective on those twists and turns. I've begun to pare away the false and inessential—my penchant for overdoing, my need to be accepted, my impulse for the rash and brash. I am getting to the nub of me, and I like what I'm finding there. The small tales in this book are meant to illustrate my progress and perhaps to help others on a similar path.

This is not a book of grand pronouncements or high-flown philosophy. Whatever wisdom I have today is the fruit of my experience and especially my mistakes. They have made me at once stronger and more humble; they are the simple lessons of my life.

Sarah Ferguson
The Duchess of York
October 15, 2002

FORGIVING THE PAST

Readers of *My Story* may recall my old foes the Grey Men, the Palace bureaucrats who found me insufficiently royal in every way: my dress, my bearing, the friends I kept. They did what they could to make my life a misery, with a strong assist from myself, of course. After leaving their milieu, I'd had no contact with any of these gentlemen for an age—until last year, when I strolled down a street in Mayfair and passed an art shop. There in the window sat an original portrait, by a well-known painter, of one of the top courtiers.

I didn't think twice. I bought the portrait and sent it to the courtier (now retired) with a simple note that I thought he might like it for his children, and I hoped he was well, and I sent my love. I didn't buy the gift to be kinder-than-thou. I simply knew that it would please him, as it would have pleased me. I would have done the same for anyone I knew.

A few days later, the mail brought the man's response. Out of respect I will paraphrase, but here is the gist of it: *I cannot believe that after all that has happened between us, you can be kind enough to do this.*

In that exchange, our history was forever altered.

For years I had stewed in my anger at all who had hurt me. Bitterness can be seductive. As long as you hold to it, you are forever wronged—and thus forever right. Over time, however, I came to realize that animosity was no good for me. It spoiled my natural optimism, made me tedious to be around. Worse yet, it kept me from learning from my errors.

When it came to the Grey Man in question, I thought about why I'd been so furious with him. Then I solved the puzzle: I was angry with *myself,* for the blunders that had prompted his rebukes. I tried to look at life from the courtier's point of view. By his own lights, he was an honest man doing his job. And if, with hindsight, he might have done it less gruffly, what did that matter now?

My first step, in sum, was to acknowledge my own trespasses. Once done, it was not so hard to forgive the Grey Man, too.

Now I see that I have no right to bear a grudge, nor any

interest in it. To lash back can only feed the old injury and any lingering self-doubt. To snub a person is to forfeit our future together. In the end, we both lose.

I do not merely rise above old wrongs; I deny them their reality. I sever my connections to darker times and circumstance. I take people with a fresh eye and an open heart, as they come to me *today*. Their old dossiers have expired. Our new story has yet to be written. By refusing to hurt another, I heal my wounds as well.

CO-PARENTING AND COMMON SENSE

*T*hrough all the storms that have tossed us, Andrew and I have kept safe what we hold most dear: our abiding friendship and the two young girls we've raised together. We've dealt with friction like everyone else, but we've always tried to put Beatrice and Eugenie first. It is a matter of common sense. Regardless of what else changes in our lives, Andrew will always be my daughters' father. In parenting we will always be partners.

As in many families, regardless of marital status, Mommy takes charge of the day-to-day, the scheduling and school affairs. Andrew, who travels the globe in the cause of British trade, knows that I do well at tracking the girls' needs. But at the same time, our parenting works because we sustain an active collaboration where it counts.

First, Andrew and I share the values we've hoped to impart to our children: integrity, forgiveness, honesty, humor, enthusiasm, grace.

Second, we spare them from our knotty grown-up problems. When we are with our daughters, separately or together, we are there *for* them, as well. We give them the attention they deserve.

Third, we hold an open discussion of any issue involving the girls. When it came time to choose their current schools, for example, we both agreed that they should go to different ones, so that each could shine in her own right. Andrew then left it to me to put the wheels in motion—to hash out with Beatrice and Eugenie exactly where they should go, to make the tours and interview the headmasters. He trusted me to find the right solution.

Fourth, we plan regular family times together. The four of us dote on our trips to the cinema Friday night. We plan at least one summer holiday together and always cheer our girls on at sports day at school.

Finally, when we disagree as parents, which isn't often, we steer clear of power plays or pressure tactics. We simply work it out together. For example, when Andrew first heard of my plan to take Beatrice to visit the HIV-positive children of St. Petersburg, he thought she was too young. Rather than stew about it, he came to me with his reservations: "What is the program? What is she going to do?" After talking to me, he came around to endorsing the trip. And after we came back, and he saw our daughter's confidence soaring, he was the first to say that the encounter had done her a world of good. In truth, he'd never been too worried, because he knew that I had her best interests at heart.

On the other hand, it was Andrew who took the lead upon the death of his grandmother last March. He brought the girls out to say good morning to the people who'd lined up to see The Queen Mother lying in state. I knew that it might be very sad and difficult for our daughters to do it, but I supported their father nonetheless.

Beatrice and Eugenie have told us, more than once, that they hope our family arrangement will stay just as it is now—just as it is pictured on the Christmas cards sent from the four of us.

Little can be guaranteed in this turbulent world of ours. But I can promise our daughters that one thing shall be constant. Their father and I shall always stand behind them, connected for all time.

EATING OUT, EATING RIGHT

Through much of my adulthood, I worshipped the false god of excess. I overspent and overdressed and over-reacted, and most of all I overate. Every restaurant was a theme park, and I had to try every ride. I had achieved that level of notoriety where chefs would eagerly send me their signature dishes and all sorts of complimentary extras. Miracles of saturated fat would fly to my table at no cost, at least monetarily.

To this day, I find enchantment in the mingling of old friends and new flavors in a public space. (I prefer the more casual establishments, where food and fun take center stage, and I don't feel conspicuous if I laugh too loud.) I delight in the look of a menu. I love the spare poetry that puts words to food, the promise of gastronomic excitement.

At the same time, I have gained a hard-earned respect for the havoc that a four-star, five-course, foie-gras-and-confit carnival can wreak on my self-discipline, my sense of well-being, and ultimately my waistline. In self-defense, I have learned to demystify the gourmet experience. I still eat very well, but I eat smart.

As with many things, it begins with a touch of extra courage to stand out from a crowd. While I respect that beautiful menu, I do not treat it as gospel. There are few fish that cannot be grilled or poached as well as sautéed, few poultry dishes that can't come without the skin. Any vegetable can be steamed; any sauce can be ordered on the side. (Once I've set the sauce or salad dressing in its place, I'll dip my fork in it before spearing the meat or fish or lettuce leaf. I'll get flavor with minimal fat.) If my custom order seems a bit bland, I'll ask for lemon juice or balsamic vinegar to jazz it up a bit. And if the chef cannot modify a rich recipe, I'll happily go back to square one and order something else.

Then there is the matter of portions and courses. In reality, the body requires only a hand-sized measure of protein to keep it well filled. (I should add that my reference point is *my* hand or *your* hand, not the platter-sized paws of Shaquille O'Neal.) There is no need for the 34-ounce porterhouse that could nourish the cello section of the New York Philharmonic.

If, despite my best-laid plans, my main course arrives oversized, I'll ask for it to be split in two, with half going straight to a doggy bag. Now I've both delivered myself from temptation and won a special lunch or dinner for the next day. If I'm *really* not hungry, I feel no pressure to order an entrée at all. I'll ask for two appetizers, or an appetizer and a salad, just enough to keep me in the flow of my companions' meal.

There is no point in going out, after all, if you're going out to say *no;* you might as well stay home with the dog and a video. There is no harm in accepting a glass of Chardonnay, or a slice of your neighbor's chicken-fried chicken, or a helping of the Quintuple-Chocolate-Bypass from the dessert tray. Who will notice or care if you have a small taste and leave the rest? By saying *yes,* you avoid an annoying third-degree about your diet plan. You separate the social (joining the party) from the personal (what you ingest).

In other words, you can have your cake and *not* eat it, too. I call it "all gong and no dinner." I take a breadstick and pass the basket. I try everything on my plate—and stop there. I make much ado about nothing, and everyone is happy, most of all me.

REACHING OUT

During my last stay in the south of France, I took to biking down a quiet road. Round a corner, I passed a little old house and, in its yard, a portly, ruddy-faced woman in a floral apron and fluffy slippers. I don't know why, exactly, but something about her intrigued me, made me want to extend myself. I waved at her as I went by, and she must have thought I was some daft tourist, because she didn't wave back.

The same thing happened the second day. But on the third day, the old woman returned a tentative wave, and by the fourth day, she nearly got out of her chair as I called out, *"Bonjour, madame!"* It became a small ritual between us. She had no idea who I was, nor when I was coming, but she seemed to be waiting for me. Once she brought her grizzled husband out with her, and they *both* waved to beat the band.

On my last day, my last ride, I took some flowers and tied them to my bike with a ribbon. I cycled down to the little house and rounded the corner—but the lady wasn't there. Disappointed, I tied the flowers to her gate as a parting gift.

Back at my house, I told Roger, the gardener, of my missed connection. He knew instantly what had happened. The old lady had a bad leg, Roger said, and walking troubled her, so she'd gone to the hospital for surgery. Each day I had passed her so blithely, not knowing that she'd been in pain.

"Who is she?" I asked.

The quiet road, Roger explained, used to be a railway. The old lady's husband was once the stationmaster, and their house was the stationmaster's house. Several times a day, whenever a train had passed, the couple would see a flurry of waves from the passengers—especially the children on board, for whom a ride was high adventure.

My bicycle, it seems, was a remembrance of locomotives past: a ghost train. As Roger said, "She has missed the trains and the waves. You brought them back to her."

By reaching out, in a way that cost me nothing, I'd given more than I had realized.

TIMING IT RIGHT

Dads was a bear for punctuality, as befit an officer in the Queen's Household Cavalry. When I was a young girl working in London and commuting home each night, my train never beat him to the village station. He'd be there on the dot, without fail.

His discipline cut both ways, however. I habitually ran late, and once I missed the train home and thought nothing of hopping the next one, an hour later. When I rang, Dads flatly refused to pick me up; he'd driven off fuming, and he wasn't coming back. I had to walk several miles before finding a taxi, a good lesson in the wages of presumption.

Unfortunately, the lesson didn't take. In my Palace days, I overstuffed my calendar with as many as 300 official engagements in a year, on top of my intensive charity work, those marathon state dinners, my early-morning flying lessons, and a pair of pregnancies. I was perpetually late in a family where timeliness was next to godliness.

My toxic habit was set. Long after I left the Royal Family, when my time was in theory more my own, I stayed hopelessly overscheduled. My stress ran off the chart. Like Alice's rabbit, I was always hurried and distracted—and like the rabbit, I never caught up. How could I enjoy one event when I was running late for the next?

Let us say I needed to leave for an engagement at 1:30. I'd be ready to go at the appointed hour—except that I'd "forgotten" to touch up my hair. It was deeper than forgetting, of course: self-sabotage in the first degree. It's oft said that lateness shows a want of respect for those waiting. But as my father once taught me, it is even more insulting to ourselves. To be late is to lose control and opportunity. By failing to set temporal boundaries, we set ourselves up to fail.

While I remain a work in progress in this area, I am getting better. I feel very proud when I'm punctual, like someone kicking an addiction, one appointment at a time. I devote my calendar to what counts—my girls, my exercise, the work that sustains us, the friends who bring us joy—and prune away the rest, so there are fewer things to be late for. I was doing a right fine job of it, in fact, until I was invited to a British Embassy dinner.

Wedgwood had booked me in North Carolina that day, and I knew it would be touch and go to make it to Washington on time. The new Sarah tries to avoid that kind of pressure, but this invitation was special. It wasn't so many years ago that a Palace worthy advised the British establishment to bar its doors to me. I was, at long last, rehabilitated. It was an offer I could not refuse.

My plane landed right on time. I was in good shape, except that I'd failed to account for Chaos Theory. For mysterious reasons, we were held on the tarmac at Reagan National for forty minutes. I sprinted through the airport in a pouring sweat, my hair curling like a Marx brother's. I charged into the ladies' room to change into my formal wear and apply makeup. Over the years, I've shaved my makeovers to five minutes flat: blusher, lip liner, and eye liner to show some effort; a black velvet scrunchie to put my hair up; deodorant and a spray of eau de toilette.

I still might have made it had the policeman driving our car not lost his way. By the time we pulled up to the embassy, I was in a full-fledged panic, my posture and poise eroded. I knew what my fellow guests would be thinking: *Typical, isn't it? She'll never change . . .* I'd lived down to my reputation. By the time I walked into the great ballroom, under a chandelier the size of Belgium, everyone else was seated—I'd missed the first course. Though I did my best to join in the spirit of things, I never quite caught up.

I'd learn two lessons that night. First, that it may be better to take a rain check than to cut one's schedule too close. Second, that most venial sins are forgivable, and most people will give you another chance. I was asked back to the embassy some months later, and for that I cleared my calendar. You may trust me when I tell you I was beautifully on time.

SURVIVING YOUR CRITICS

*F*rom the moment I got engaged to Andrew, I became a natural resource for England's many tabloids. At the start, when I was still a cross between Mary Poppins and Cinderella, the front pages all hailed the FABULOUS, FANTAS-TIC FERGIE, the GREAT-FUN FERGIE who would sponge the mildew from the Palace walls.

Soon enough, however, I slipped from favor. The stories took on a different cast: FAT, FRUMPY, FREEBIE FERGIE FAILS AGAIN!

As my star plummeted, Fleet Street became ever more creative. One article claimed that 82% WOULD RATHER SLEEP WITH GOAT THAN FERGIE! (I'm afraid that I was far enough gone to question the judgment of the other 18 percent.)

But the headline that took first prize, set above a fearsome photograph, was a crudely effective play on words: DUCHESS OF PORK! Featured in one of the heavier-breathing tabloids, it was for me unforgettable. Years later, when the editor invited me to a luncheon roundtable with some lawyers and bankers and people in the news, it still haunted me.

After a pleasant meal and chat, I was taken round to meet the newspaper's staff. We stopped before the desk of a jovial, middle-aged man who greeted me like an old friend.

"Oh, I'm quite excited," he said. "It's lovely to meet you because basically we know each other so well."

Here, I was told, was the talented fellow who had written those striking headlines. I stood dumbfounded as I shook his hand. *This* was the man who had kidnapped my sleep and composure for days on end? *This* was my great enemy—this round-bellied, balding chap with a quick and hearty laugh? I felt like Dorothy after the Great and Terrible Oz had lost his curtain.

I told him, "You caused me great distress, you know."

He seemed puzzled: "Oh dear, I didn't mean to."

Before long I was joking with the chap who'd given me so much grief. I asked how he would handle a wayward celebrity then in the news. "Okay," he said, "what rhymes with ———?"

And I thought, *It really is as simple as that.* The headline writer obviously bore me no malice and never had. He was paid to be clever, end of story. Where I once took his every pun so personally, he'd invested no more emotion in them than he would in his tie clasp or his carburetor.

The man mused, "It's like history, isn't it? We've been together for fifteen years, and now we're together here today."

Indeed. It *was* history, truly yesterday's news. It occurred to me that we survive our critics by knowing that their agendas, at heart, may have little to do with us.

LAUGHING OUT LOUD

M y confirmation was a big day for a little girl. My rela
tives sat stiff and proud in the pew. The service was aus-
terely sublime. The whole affair went off perfectly, in
fact—until I came back from the altar and broke into a
huge, beaming smile, then an audible siege of giggles.

Mum was slightly mortified: "Can't you ever take anything seriously?"

The odd thing was, I *did* take religion seriously; I had
deep faith when I was thirteen. But I couldn't help myself.
Something struck me as awfully funny that day—the
hushed reverence, my starched white dress, I cannot say
for sure. My church giggles grew louder and louder, and the
more I tried to tame them, the worse they got, until the
Church of England must have had doubts about my
prospects for salvation.

(Years later, I was gratified to find that the Archbishop of Canterbury was on my side. As the late Robert Runcie once said, "Laughter is one of God's greatest gifts. To reach sanctity is to be able to laugh at our mortality and take only God seriously.")

I still find life to be funny above all. Humor is an intrinsic part of my day and laughter my preferred therapy, a shot of adrenaline straight to my brain. If I don't have a good dose of *Friends* or Billy Connolly or the like, I feel deprived, as though I've missed a night's sleep.

Recently I was asked to inaugurate the *Kansas City Star*'s speaker series at their local opera house. I didn't realize how big a deal it was until I saw the billboards about town, my name emblazoned like the featured diva's in a new *Traviata*. I'd given scores of speeches before but never in a setting quite like this. The hall was exquisite and formal and intimidating. I stomped up and down behind the velvet curtain, peeking out at the packed house. For a terrible moment, I was seized by opera giggles.

I finally went on stage and scanned about, and everyone looked quite grave, and I thought, *Ooh, this is going to be a tough one.* I decided I had but one recourse: to make light of the situation and puncture my own balloon. So I said, "Here I am. I suppose you want me to sing an aria, because that is what normally happens here, isn't it? Well, that is bad luck, because you don't want to get that. It would not be pretty."

(In truth, I cannot sing a note, notwithstanding the rumor that I'd been offered a part in the Broadway production of *Jekyll & Hyde*. Had I been cast, they would have changed it to *Run & Hyde*.)

The audience laughed and relaxed, and so did I. Even a middling joke can chop a venue down to size, and suddenly I was in an overgrown parlor with a thousand or two of my closest friends. Our question-and-answer session turned almost giddy.

As vital as humor is to me today, there was a time when it saved my life. During my dark days in the Royal Family, I had to laugh if not to cry, or worse. From the start, humor lay at the core of my staunch friendship with Diana. In public we'd poke fun at the pomposity around us; in private we'd banter in rapid fire, to see who had the quicker wit. We were great ones for practical joking, as well. A week before my marriage, we staged a wild hen night, donning gray wigs and authentic policewoman outfits, and wound up arrested by the boys in blue for creating a disturbance outside Buckingham Palace.

The memory I cherish most, though, is Diana's laughter at our regular Sunday lunches, when it was just family, and we could be ourselves. When Diana really laughed, it was very deep, from the bottom of her stomach. I miss that sound terribly. There was nothing like it to keep my sadness at bay—to remind me that the world was not such a bad place, as long as you didn't take it too seriously.

KEEPING RITUALS

Children need the structure of routine, the comfort of the expected—and a legacy of ritual to pass on to their own sons and daughters. In my girlhood, Mum would organize our annual ski trips and the family Christmases and the most elaborate, fanciful birthday parties in the Western Hemisphere. On any given weekend, she'd throw together an outing for me and my school chums: swimming, the cinema, the circus.

My favorite ritual with Mum might seem a modest one: lunch at Fortnum & Mason. I'd order the identical meal each time, a ham salad followed by a trio of sorbets. I always had one scoop each of lemon, mandarin, and raspberry; the sameness was part of the fun of it.

Dads wasn't so skilled in the domestic arts, but he, too, recognized the value of ritual. When I was small, he'd shower me each year with birthday cards signed by suspicious sources: the cat, the garage, the apple tree. After Mum, and then my sister, Jane, moved away, Dads took on Christmas stocking duty. The year I passed my driving test, he stuffed a pillowcase with sponges and antifreeze and de-icer fluid, with all the price tags left on. The routine had been altered, but the ritual remained!

Now I try to nurture our own rich store of tradition. Beatrice and Eugenie look forward all week to our Sunday family lunches and all summer to the last day before school begins. That's when we go to London for lunch at an Italian restaurant called Santini, then to shop for new pencil cases and school shoes.

When I am home with my girls, I still read them a story and put them to bed and tell them I love them, even though they are nearly as tall as I. At tea we always have sausage rolls when there are guests. Every Easter the three of us go to someplace warm, a tradition we've vowed to keep forever.

And every Mother's Day, without fail, Beatrice and Eugenie bring me breakfast in bed. It is a very special breakfast of my old-time favorites: soft-boiled eggs and toast cut into hearts and stars, laden down with so much butter that it's gasping for air. Then my daughters jump on the bed, and the tea slops all over, and we are lost in laughter and love. It is the best of traditions—as we keep it intact, so it keeps us happy and secure.

REJECTING REJECTION

A few years back, a leading fashion magazine called to say they wanted to shoot me for their cover. At first I turned them down; I wasn't up to it. My mother had just died, and I felt wretched. I'd binged my way through the mourning in Argentina, and though my weight was perfectly healthy, a third less than my peak in my Palace days, I was ten pounds too heavy for the realm of couture. I warned them that I wasn't tiny-sized, that they'd be dealing with a normally proportioned thirty-eight-year-old woman.

The editor insisted. "We *really* want you for the cover," she said. "You'll be marvelous! You'll be fabulous!"

Against my better judgment, I gave in. I was hugely flattered, of course, but it was more than that. The renowned photographer they'd assigned to me had once worked with Diana, the most beautiful woman I have ever known. I thought, *Diana did it—just maybe I can do it, too.* After all the public sneerings at my figure, the microscopic scrutiny of my every bump, I had finally arrived. When you've put your ugly duckling days behind you, it is only natural to yearn to flex those gorgeous swan wings.

They *wanted* me. They wanted *me!*

But from the moment I arrived at the shoot, I sensed that they didn't want me, after all. A set of orange extensions was glued to my scalp; my hair was too curly, and there wasn't enough of it. My stylist was the classic Tough Old Broad, a veteran of many a fitting-room war. She took one look at me and removed her cigarette, stubbed it out, and replaced it in her mouth with a dozen pins.

"Come on, get in," she muttered, as I stared skeptically at a Vera Wang dress, size ten. "We'll have to pin it, because your hips are too wide, and they don't make it any bigger than this. And oh yes, put on those panty hose with the Lycra bits to squeeze it all in."

It was all so uncaring, so humiliating. I felt like the Elephant Man as they chased him into the bowels of Victoria Station: "I am not an animal! I am a human being!" As my handlers pinned and strapped and patched me, I wanted to scream: *I am not a model! I am a human being!*

The photographer's assistants came in to check the camera set-up and turn on the synthesized catwalk music.

(Please, sir, a little Brahms?) Then in marched the great man himself. He scanned the field like a general rushed to the front, and then it was: *Flash! Bye! Gone!*

When I saw the proofs, I thought all hands had done a remarkable job. The chosen photograph didn't look anything like me, of course. It looked like a very stylish mannequin with half her face obscured by hair extensions, à la Morticia Addams.

I heard nothing more for weeks, until the day the magazine was to appear. I was at breakfast in my hotel, about to leave to tape a full hour on *Oprah*, a challenge that takes every ounce of confidence I can muster. My publicist took a call and passed the phone to me. It was the editor.

"You know, the pictures are lovely," she said. "But I don't think we'll use them for the cover, because you look a bit *weighty.*"

They'd use Madonna, instead.

I felt smacked in the face. My old, buried personae swam up to the surface: the Willing Victim, the Apology Girl. As I thanked the editor for the opportunity, calmly and politely, inside I was roiling: *Of course they don't want to use you, how ridiculous to think you could measure up . . .*

But rather quickly I righted my ship. I was hurt and disappointed, no question, but I also knew that I was healthy and fit. I actually *liked* the way I looked, and my opinion mattered more than the editor's. As I gazed at the cover proofs, at my tortured facsimile, I saw that the fashion world was not mine and never would be. I can be no one's tabula rasa; I have lived too much to fit another's mold. Models are objects of fantasy, and my life is too rooted in the real.

The irony is that I now *am* a size ten and could slide into that Vera Wang dress with ease. But I would say no to that cover today, were the offer to come. I would turn it down because I am still *weighty*, a person of some substance, and weighty I shall remain.

FINDING EMPATHY

My *typical day on tour:* I'm up at 4:00, a dark and empty hour I've learned to savor, because it still belongs to me. I go straight to my bound notebook, where I write every single thing I must do that day: "Fax letter to girls"; "Write speech for meeting"; "Speak to UK office."

I climb onto my stationary bicycle, where I remember how to breathe. Then a quick working-girl's breakfast of egg-white omelet and fruit and tea, and some lightning hair and makeup, and I'm off . . . to the local TV studio for a four-hour Weight Watcher satellite tour, to be beamed about the land in fifteen-minute increments. It is grueling work. I sit in a black room under a spotlight, answering the same questions while trying to be original. Then I hop in the car to shuttle to various radio stations for more interviews. Then we move on to my meeting, where I give my speech and meet people afterwards—sometimes hundreds of them—and sign their books.

And all of that happens before lunch.

It would be a fraying schedule, except that I am refreshed by what I do. When I speak to people in Weight Watchers, I am simply a woman with a weight problem, though it might be in remission. We relate to one another as fellow pilgrims on a mountain trail—with candor and empathy, and the pluck that comes from perseverance.

My own struggles remain all too vivid to me. The feeling that you've let yourself down. The urge to overcompensate in other areas (working, spending, joking), so that no one will look at just *you,* the self-loathing person you are. The deadening sense that you will never get over that mountain and therefore might as well eat, and so the mountain gets higher and higher . . .

Without support, the trek would be too perilous to bear. Weight Watchers gives me a cohort where no one is looking and judging. I love the opportunity to share our small triumphs, those two steps forward for each one back, and to hearten those who may be flagging. At a recent gathering in Albany—a *Super* Meeting, with more than 2,000 people—my eyes were somehow drawn to the middle of the crowd, to a woman in a green track suit. Her brow was furrowed, her mouth etched in a frown. She appeared to be having a perfectly miserable time.

I saw myself in that woman, in all her apparent anguish. In my not-so-distant past, I had felt very much the same, nearly every single day: unworthy of attention, a chronic disappointment, a worthless case.

I took that woman on as my challenge for the morning. I aimed my talk straight at her, to see if my best jokes or sad bits might get some reaction. Nothing worked. The longer I went on, the harder I tried, the more despondent she seemed.

At the close of each meeting, I choose someone to receive my gift of Little Red, a doll that reflects the spirit of my charity work in America. I wanted to give the doll that day to the woman in the green suit, but I was almost afraid to do it. Did she hate my speech? Would she run the other way?

In the end, I followed my intuition and reached out to her. The woman—her name was Mary—came up on stage and promptly burst into tears. She said, "Oh my God, you don't know what this means to me."

Indeed, I didn't know, but I'd sensed it might be important to single her out. Later on, a Weight Watchers leader told me, "That was the one woman in the audience who needed to be made to feel special!" I learned that Mary was mired in troubles that had left her demoralized. She was on the brink of dropping out of the program, until Little Red brought her back.

That encounter made my whole tour. More strongly than ever, I felt that my work had real meaning, whatever its stresses and strains. I was eager to go through it all again the next day. Who knew whose lives I might touch, or who might touch mine, if only we could find a link between us?

NAMING NAMES

*I*f I have a knack for small talk, it's because I often don't talk much at all. Whenever I meet people for the first time, I assume that they have at least one great story to tell and that it's my job to find it. In asking people about themselves, I've scored twice. I've put them on their favorite subject, which helps them shine. They teach, and I learn, and most often I get the better of the deal.

Small talk, after all, is the common currency of social life. Far more than simple courtesy, it broadens our exposure, exposes new worlds. Probe well enough and one can always find common ground, even in foreign territory. When I went to a Wedgwood factory floor in northern England, for instance, I heard one of the men groaning, "Oh, no."

"Excuse me," I said. "What do you mean, 'Oh, no'?" It turned out he'd been expecting a different Fergie—Alex Ferguson, the manager of the legendary soccer club Manchester United. "I'm very sorry," I said. "You've got *me*, and you'll have to lump it." I made sport of the man's confusion until everyone was laughing, and then I asked him which team he supported, and why he thought Sir Alex was such a good chap. Given an opening, the soccer fan led me well. Instead of getting defensive or flustered, I'd relaxed and actually learned something.

Listening, I fear, is a lost art. Rule number one is to let a person's story flow and not to interrupt it with one of your own. If you let it go far enough, you'll inevitably find points you have in common: children, schools, hobbies, homes. But when people preempt the speaker and compulsively shift the topic to themselves, they remind me of the old joke: *Enough about me, let's talk about you . . . What do you think of me?*

Whenever I meet someone new, I'm ready to make a game of it. I find a physical trait or piece of apparel—a goatee, a colorful tie, a pair of tasseled loafers—and I visually link it to the bearer's name. I make the image humorous (at least to me) or even ridiculous, so I won't forget. If the name is at all unusual, I ask the person to spell it and picture the letters in my head. Then I use it repeatedly in conversation: *Tell me, Kevin . . .*

As a wise person once said: There is no sweeter sound to a man than that of his own name. It lends warmth and familiarity to the newest acquaintanceships; I am no longer merely speaking but speaking to *you*. If someone hangs back at a Weight Watcher meeting, I'll march up to her and say, "What's your name? Vivian? I see that you've got a camera, Vivian. Don't you want to take a picture? Come on, girls, help Vivian, we'll make it a group shot." Vivian can't hide anymore, because now I know *who she is*. We're connected.

The best trick for names is no trick at all. It is simply to get to know someone, until their name automatically follows. At our Spanish dinner, for example, some simple reconnaissance confirmed that Kevin was married and his spouse was at the table. Not knowing the wife's name, I said, "So, Kevin, which is your sweetheart?"

"Sweetheart?" he said, laughing. "Why, Ann and I have been married for thirty years!" He pointed her out, and I turned to include her in our conversation. She had on a knockout pearl necklace.

"Really, Kevin," I said. (*Kevin-goatee, Ann-necklace,* I was thinking.) "How have you managed to stay together so long? What is your secret?" Then we were off and running. Kevin and I were no longer strangers—we were on a first-name basis, and that made all the difference.

MINDING MANNERS

My mother came from the Irish gentry. A perfect lady, she showed by her example that good manners meant more than using the right fork. After a lunch or dinner at someone's home, she would lead me into the kitchen to thank the cook—every single time. Mum gave the same smile to everyone. Her courtesy ran bone-deep, but her style was all sparkle and spontaneity, in tune with the company and occasion.

The importance of manners struck home when I was twenty and set off with a friend on a New World adventure. We were flat broke by the time we reached Squaw Valley and took what jobs we could find. In the morning I cleaned the dormitories at a youth hostel, where my best efforts went unnoticed. In the evening I waited tables at an apple strudel shop, which I found more fulfilling—not only for the free strudels (a short-term addiction, I must admit), but for every "please" and "thank you" that kept my spirit afloat. They are small words and undervalued; they are the coin of respect.

With my own daughters, now fourteen and twelve, I try to follow my mother's approach to manners: to be constant in principle but flexible in practice. As members of the Royal Family, Beatrice and Eugenie will be on parade one day and flinging potato chips with their friends the next. To help them make sense of it all, I've devised a three-tier system of manners, with descending levels of formality.

Our A manners represent our top form, impeccably correct, for the more formal public places, from church to Palace visits with Granny. My girls know that they will be dressing their best and arriving promptly. They will stay alert to what's happening, even if an event turns tedious, and will do as they're told without fuss.

Tier B is where Beatrice and Eugenie spend most of their public lives—in outings with their mother and father, at concerts and movies and gatherings with school friends and their families. I love to see my daughters enjoy themselves, but I also see to it that they treat people respectfully. In a restaurant, our first rule is to sit properly, head held high, always ready with a smile. My girls must be courteous to one another and polite to the restaurant staff, whether we're at the Ritz or McDonald's.

We need to unwind as much as the next clan, which is where Tier C comes into play. When we're at home together, and especially at Sunday lunch, anything can—and usually will—happen. There might be an uproarious game of charades or some silly practical joke. When we're not in the mood for an elaborate meal, we'll create some "incredible edible" concoction. (Our current favorite: prosciutto, cream cheese, and apricot jam on white bread.)

Even at our most informal, though, I'll take the time to set a pretty table, just as Mum did, with her linens and bits of china and something clever from the cupboard or garden. I'll try to bring some magic to an ordinary day, to remind us all that the soul of good manners is to prize each other's company.

In sum: We use Tier A to honor, Tier B to show respect, Tier C to relax and be ourselves. We use the rules to navigate so we can savor the ride.

AGING WELL

I don't often admit it, but I am beginning to feel my age—not that I'm making concessions to it. My stamina, my greatest asset, is undiminished. I still put in fourteen-hour days on the road, and then, when my young staff is pining for a bath and bed, I head out for dinner at full throttle.

It is only at the evening's end that the weight of fatigue bears down on me. My legs hurt; my back aches. After all the years of pushing my body to the nth degree, my body has begun to push back.

At those leaden moments, I boost my morale by remembering the women in my family, the ones who thought aging happened to everyone else. My mother's mother—the redoubtable, chain-smoking dynamo we knew as Grummy—suffered a crushed pelvis in a riding accident as a young woman. She lived with great pain through most of her life. The shortest walk was an ordeal for her.

But Grummy never complained. She was too busy laughing and dancing her little jigs and chomping into the hard chocolate bars that jarred loose her false teeth. In my teens and her seventies, when I urgently needed a female sounding board, she showed no reluctance in discussing the facts of life. Well into her eighties, she tended her garden and made her colorful tapestries, including a self-portrait with a cigarette hanging from her lips. Grummy was proof positive that while bodies will age, minds can stay young and active forever.

My mother was past fifty when my stepfather, Hector Barrantes, died in Argentina. They say that tragedy ages people, but Mum proved otherwise. She took over the running of their ranch, where they bred polo ponies, the same way she did everything else—with her Irish spirit of light-hearted adaptability and a well-honed sense of the ridiculous. She spent her days among young ranch hands and spoke their language. She wore blue jeans and kept her hair long. To the day she died—much too young, at sixty-one—she remained as bold and lively as I recalled her in my childhood. She was like a light in a dark room.

Some of my greatest inspirations are ageless women with young spirits, like Lauren Bacall or Shirley MacLaine or Tina Turner. Like them, I feel that I have just started my journey. With apologies to Descartes: I think I am young, therefore I am. I stay young by taking care of myself. I eat well and keep fit, and on the beach I wear floppy hats and layers of sunscreen and sunglasses at all times. (When I crave the bronzed look, I apply a browning agent—a fake tan—and for two weeks I can rival George Hamilton.)

I stay young by reliving my youth through my children, by steeping myself in their interests and concerns.

Most of all, I stay young by doing young things. I might ride a horse across the Arabian desert, as I did when I was thirty-six. Or dance till six in the morning, or play an extra set of tennis, or push my mind with the Sunday crossword puzzle. It is all a matter of willpower, of going the extra mile, and of knowing how far you want to go.

I do not fear old age; what I fear is regret. I am passionate about living, I feel driven to seize every moment, for the clock never stops.

And when I am seventy and have squeezed the juice from life and drunk it down, I'll still be galloping my horse, and no one will catch me. I'll have my dogs and my cameras on a wild farm in the middle of nowhere. I will follow the advice of the late Ashley Montagu: "The idea is to die young as late as possible."

I see myself as a very young old woman, to the end.

TAKING WHAT LIFE
GRANTS YOU

I met Igor in 1994, at a function for Children in Crisis, my international charity. Brought to live in England by Chernobyl Children's Lifeline, he had a loving foster mother and took everything else as it came. I found him amazing for his friendly gusto; he was a fantastic little boy.

Igor's only fault was bad timing. He'd been conceived in 1986, shortly before the worst nuclear accident in history. His mother lived just 40 miles south of Chernobyl. She had no idea what the disaster had wrought until the boy was born—with no right arm, and legs stunted and fanned in the shape of fishtails.

The authorities took Igor from his mother when he was two days old, and he spent the first seven years of his life in a hospital ward in Belarus, longing for a second arm and the independence it might bring to him.

I invited Igor to my children's next party. I suppose that I wanted to remind Beatrice and Eugenie of their good fortune in life and to see beyond superficial differences in people. But Igor was much more than a lesson plan. He was the perfect guest, happy to meet and mingle. Having learned to walk quite well, he followed along behind the other children. He played every game. We enjoyed him so much that he became a regular at birthdays and Christmastime.

When we organized an outing to Planet Hollywood in London, Igor was thrilled to sit on Sylvester Stallone's motorbike. But he was no less excited with his hamburger and chips—the whole experience was a magic carpet ride for him. It didn't matter that everyone else at his table had four working appendages. He never saw himself as an object of pity. He was happy because he was Igor!

I began to notice something interesting. Whenever I spent time with Igor, I felt more optimistic. My own petty obstacles seemed less daunting, my dilemmas more soluble. At my advanced age, I was learning what Igor already knew intuitively. If we do our best within our limits, if we meet our setbacks with resilience, we cannot be denied.

Not long after we met Igor, he was fitted with a prosthetic right arm. His great dream had come true. One day he gingerly picked up a pen with his new limb and sketched a self-portrait. "Look," he said with pride, "it's Igor with two arms!"

He had always been whole in spirit. Now his body was catching up to his soul, and who would stop him?

DRESSING TO THRILL

I'd been at odds with my clothes for as long as I could remember. In my pre-Royal days, I dressed as I pleased in a sort of *haute* Salvation Army. My old style wouldn't do, however, after I married Andrew. Desperate to please, straining to emulate Diana's panache, I assembled the Wardrobe from Hell. I was drowning in big hats and frills and bows in all the wrong places; I became, as the papers were quick to note, a Fashion Disaster.

In an effort to learn from my mistakes, I gradually became more tailored and conservative. I played safe, did my best to hide my bottom—and still I foundered. As late as 1996, Mr. Blackwell named me the sixth-worst-dressed woman in the world. While I dismissed the man as a misogynist, I knew that he wasn't all wrong. I was dressing defensively. I never felt that anything quite fit me, in line or in spirit.

It was only quite recently that I felt fit and trim and confident enough to grow bolder. Now, at last, I know my assets: red hair, large eyes, long legs. I rely on classic suits with skirts that show off my "pins." At the same time, I am also open to a touch of flamboyance, like my belt buckle with the Union Jack and Stars and Stripes. In spirit, I suppose, I'm following the women in Vichy France who flouted the German occupiers by going out in public with an extra touch of color: their small cry of rebellion.

Last May I attended a Children in Crisis fundraiser in the City of London, Britain's Wall Street, a place where men's suits run the gamut from charcoal to black. I knew that I'd be expected to turn up in a long-sleeved black velvet dress, something inoffensive and virtually invisible.

But the very idea made me want to howl. I'd gone the black-velvet route at one affair too many. I'd worked hard on my figure, and at last I had nothing to hide. I thought to myself, *Children in Crisis is my charity, and this is my party, and I'll tie-dye if I want to!*

I didn't quite tie-dye, but I found the next best thing: a curvy, sleeveless, scooped-neck, black-and-cobalt sequined gown by Amanda Wakely. For an exclamation point, I added a stunning beaded choker with little glass drops. All in all, it was quite a bold stroke, especially for one with a notorious past in the fashion department.

I suppose I've come to learn the point of fashion—to *enhance* through attire, to project the person I know myself to be. As it turned out, my sequins made a great splash at the fundraiser, even drew some good reviews in the press. (*Where's Fergie gone?* the tabloids wondered, now that there was less of me.) But to be honest, I didn't dwell so much upon how I was received, not like I once did. I didn't care who else liked the gown or not. I was dressing for *me,* pleasing myself; I was proud of how I looked.

I wore that gown for the thrill of it and felt perfectly right, inside and out.

CORRESPONDING IN STYLE

As a graduate of Queens Secretarial College, class of '77, I am a good-enough typist. For some time my friends and associates had been telling me that I must start to use e-mail, "because it's so much easier and we can get to you so much faster."

Innocent that I am, I bought a laptop computer and carted it with me on holiday, when my girls could teach me how to use it. I thought it would be a low-stress opportunity to get up to speed with the civilized world.

It was one of the great mistakes of my life. I had no idea what I was getting into.

On the first morning, I plugged in the machine and dutifully combed through my correspondence, e-mailing this one and that one. *This isn't so bad,* I thought. I'd just finished my last letter and thought I was at liberty—until I checked my "New Mail" box and found five fresh replies to what I'd just written!

As a person who likes to have her desk clear, I set about replying to the replies. Soon it was past noon, and I hadn't yet been with my children on the beach. I felt rushed and out of sorts. By saving time with technology, I'd lost half my day! To retrieve the odd millisecond, I found myself adapting that hideous computerese—typing *u* for *you, r* for *are.* I stopped bothering with punctuation or the shift key. After crafting my last reply *(truly yrs S.),* I snatched up my hat and my suntan oil and was nearly out the door, when some strange compulsion led me to tap NEW MAIL one more time, just in case.

I was aghast. There were *eight* new messages staring back at me, some of them replies to my original batch of e-mails, others replies to my replies. I skimmed through them and saw that they were little things, like most of what we say to one another. No great harm would have come to mailer or mailee had I seen them a week later.

The back-and-forthing was too thick and fast; I felt like the sorcerer's apprentice at war with too many mops. It struck me that I'd long been dubious about modern modes of communication, going back to the time that I pitched a balky manual typewriter through a second-story window at secretarial school. I just wanted to express myself, and the keys kept sticking and getting in my way, and finally I could not bear it anymore. (Brazenly, I did the same to a replacement machine.)

Now it came down to the computer or me. I pulled the plug, but my New Mail still lay there unopened, in silent accusation. The computer had gone to battery! I took the battery out, yet still the screen glowed. Reserve battery! I was hunting for a claw hammer when Beatrice came in for a drink and stayed my trembling arm . . .

The truth is that I *like* to await the postman. I want to be accessible to the people I care about, but I need to give my words consideration. If a matter is urgent, I'll pick up the phone or jump in a car. Otherwise, I would rather take my time with a heavy pen and a sheet of good bond.

A correspondence, I believe, is different from a conversation. It needs the right pace for reflection, in both directions—it cannot be dashed off. With our patience comes precision, and more. When we write in our own hand, we are more apt to add nuance and inflection with the occasional smear of ink. Our words gain resonance. They go further, last longer; they cannot be deleted with the punch of a key.

Though slower in arriving, they are well worth the wait.

SPEAKING OUT

Sixteen years ago, when I was first thrust into public life, I had no clue about formal speaking. I felt petrified whenever the duty called, but I knew I had to get on with it—there was no way out.

To improve, I began observing people around me who were good at it, Andrew in particular. I watched for every detail—how he stood, how he used his hands and eyes. I monitored his cadence and how calmly he spoke, never rushing. I saw that he took a big, deep breath before he went on, and that seemed to settle him. In particular, I saw how he established a rapport with his listeners. Regardless of his subject, Andrew didn't hide his personality or humor. His listeners were reacting to more than his words or his title; they were responding to *him*.

The turning point in my speaking career came in 1997, when I survived one of the great endurance tests: a North American lecture tour for Unique Lives and Experiences. Following the lead of Margaret Thatcher and Barbara Walters, I took the stage in seven cities in ten days. Each speech was to run at least seventy-five minutes, the duration of a one-act play.

How could I possibly fill the time? Who would want to sit and listen to *me* for so long? I sensed that I needed somehow to connect with my audience—to converse with them, not lecture them. At my kickoff engagement in Manitoba, I left my script behind me, for the first of many times, and told the story of my through-the-looking-glass life.

Something wonderful happened. I could feel my listeners set off with me on our voyage together. I gave my whole heart to that audience. When I was done, and the last question answered, they stood and applauded and gave me love back. The tour convinced me that my best presentations were the most spontaneous, the ones where I find a rhythm—a call-and-response, almost—with the people in the seats. I began noting where the audience laughed or clapped or paid closest attention. I came to realize that a good speech is not a soliloquy but a dialogue.

Since then I've stopped writing my talks out altogether, relying on bullet points instead. And if I pause or stammer now and then, that's okay, too. I'm just not a letter-perfect person, and everyone seems okay with that, even my elegant friends at Wedgwood. I know that I'm giving a performance with its own life and momentum, and it cannot be entirely rehearsed.

Most of all, I've learned to speak for *me*, to trust my point of view—to be a first-rate Sarah Ferguson instead of a second-hand, third-rate "expert." Several years ago, when I was invited to Milan for a U.N. forum on the refugee crisis in the Balkans, I had no idea I would be speaking, much less in such distinguished company. My panel mates were all doctors or scientists or agency heads, with alphabets of initials after their names. Each one held forth with great authority, as they knew their subject forward and back.

I nearly crumpled when it came to me—what could I possibly add? Damning the torpedoes, I stood up and said, "Well, here I am today, and you might want to know what on earth I'm going to talk about. We've heard all the information and statistics, and the one thing I can bring to this subject is emotion. I want to tell you about a mother who was shot while breast-feeding her baby in Kosovo"—I provided a few spare details—"and isn't that why we're all here?"

I left it at that and sat down to a strong reception. Afterwards the experts came up to thank me. I think they liked it that they hadn't heard from *The Duchess of York,* but from a mother who spoke out for another. I hadn't needed many words that day, but they were *my* words, and that's what counted.

ACCEPTING A COMPLIMENT

When I was a child, Dads drummed it into me not to be selfish. To resist the demon of self-absorption, I was not to talk or think much of myself. And I was never to fish for compliments or accept them if offered. Flattery was food for egotism, best deflected like some inappropriate gift. *You are too kind . . .*

It was the perfect code for one with no self-esteem. Well into adulthood, I never stopped deflecting. Nor did I ever stop to think that I might be offending the source of the praise as well as myself. When I climbed more than 19,000 feet to the top of Polkade in the Himalayas, I laid all credit to my Sherpa guides. When I went 26 miles in the saddle across the desert in Qatar, it was the *horse's* great feat, not the rider's.

Then, a few years back, I traveled to South Africa for an audience with Nelson Mandela, a particular hero of mine. I admired Mandela for his loyalty to a just cause, but also for his humility and forgiveness. Here is a man imprisoned for twenty-eight years, yet he emerged from jail without bitterness. He had no scores to settle, no agenda save one: to heal his bleeding country.

Mandela received me with grace; I felt uplifted simply to meet him. After our talk, he took my hand, and we went outside to face the world's media, including a live television feed to Britain. To my astonishment, my host introduced me as his "really good friend." Then he added, "This lady is always welcome in my house." Coming from such a source, those words were undeflectable. They came straight from Mandela's humanity, his transcendence— any question of flattery was absurd. And so they pierced the hardened walls of my modesty, and tears poured down my face. As soon as the press conference ended, I knew instantly who I needed to call. "Dads!" I cried. "The greatest person in the world just said I'm not such a bad old stick!"

Then I got my second surprise of the day, one that moved me even more than the first. Dads said, "I've always wanted a person of huge standing to support you publicly and say what a good person you are." He added that he'd wanted to tell the world exactly that for many years—but who would heed a father about his daughter?

In that moment I saw through the years of Dads's gruffness and to how much he'd loved me all the while. I truly heard what he said and believed every word of it. I *accepted* his words, in full, and whispered my thanks. Dads was paying me his highest compliment, better late—so much, much better—than never.

CHOOSING BATTLES

Like all proper British young ladies, I was taught to turn the other cheek. My training served me well when I became a public figure, and so a public target. I came to appreciate the need to pick my battles wisely—and usually to take the blow and walk away, no matter how tempting the call to arms.

For close to a decade now, a former business associate has painted a crosshair on my back. A relic from a more vulnerable time in my life, he has made his name by furnishing private information about me to the tabloids. I fired back in the press once or twice, until I saw that I was only making it worse. I learned to bite my tongue. More to the point, I refused to get upset and distracted by the man's latest "revelations." While he was stuck in the past, I had detached and moved on.

Though it isn't easy, I've taken the same tack with media coverage in general. If you respond, you only give the story legs for a second day. Besides, the newspaper will always have the last word.

This past September, however, I made an exception. It began when a prominent columnist deconstructed a photograph of my family in a Spanish airport, en route back to Britain. Seizing upon my look of agitation, the tabloid man concluded that I was scolding Andrew for not hauling more of the luggage. With remarkable psychic powers, he went on to interpret Beatrice's look of distress as evidence that this "was no one-off disagreement. Her eyes are downcast, as if to say: 'Oh dear, there they go again.'"

The column was riddled with inaccuracies, down to the date of Beatrice's birthday and the clothes I wore that day. (In fact, they included a Gap T-shirt and shoes from Next, rather less trendy and expensive than the writer surmised.) But most galling were its conclusions about Andrew and me—that "no matter how 'amicable' their relationship may appear on the surface, it is borne along on an undercurrent of bitterness and recrimination. . . . It is 'for the good of the children' that they continue to maintain the façade of togetherness. . . . There is a hefty price to be paid for this emotional subterfuge, however."

When we came across the column at breakfast, on the

morning of the first day of school, my initial thought was to leave it as fish-and-chip paper. But Beatrice has reached the age of strong opinions. The piece appalled her, and she said, "We cannot let this go! We must do something about it!" Confronted with my daughter's hurt and anger, I saw how this wasn't the usual hit-and-run about something I'd said or done or worn. The columnist had crossed the line. He had attacked our integrity as a family; he could not be allowed to get away with it.

In a way, he had chosen the battle for me.

I settled on crafting a response, purely as a mother—not a letter to the editor, but a full-fledged rebuttal to be played on the news pages. Rather than "defend" my arrangement with Andrew, I went on the offensive. (When protecting my young, I am ferocious.) After pointing to a few of the columnist's more careless errors, I marveled at his powers of divination, that he could glance at a snapshot and concoct from it the most intricate scenario. I noted that my airport distress had to do with my cousin, who'd been with us on the trip; she had a grumbling appendix, and I wasn't sure she was fit to fly. Beatrice, meanwhile, was reacting to a camera being shoved in her face, an intrusion she bears gracefully but does not pretend to enjoy. Finally, I challenged the assumption that divorced parents who live in harmony must be involved in "emotional subterfuge," and the malicious implication that we are damaging our children along the way. I held accountable the "influential commentators who know almost nothing about the particular arrangements they are analyzing with conviction."

My little volley had more impact than I could have hoped, in part because I'd never written anything like it before. While the offending tabloid spiked my response, two others printed it in full. Even better, the broadsheets took up the debate and sharply questioned such arrogant judging of people in the public eye. I had beaten the columnist on his own turf, on a matter that really mattered to me. I had chosen my battle well.

TRUSTING OUR CHILDREN

*I*n my view, teenagers are the most underrated and ma
ligned people on this earth. Nothing annoys me more than
bossy, hypercritical parents who seem bent on forgetting
that they too were once sixteen—that they too once
slouched around and had spots on their face and always
seemed to be doing something wrong. Our young people
can't take a breath without being warned of the dangers of
drugs or smoking or sex or the latest song lyric. But where
is the empathy for these creatures in transition, these per-
colating adults?

My own teenager, Beatrice, is an old soul with a very
clear look on life, to the point where I rely on her advice.
She absolutely *knows* things, without a grown-up's equivo-
cation, and was born to be responsible. (This may be
damning with faint praise, but she's a sight more depend-

able than her mother.) She goes to Sunday night choir practice on the dot, even when I entice her to play hooky, and I love that about her.

I believe in both my girls and try to show it in the day-to-day. In Spain last summer, as Andrew and I kept a dinner date, we freed the girls to their own dinner with our friends' children. We were having so much fun that we'd stopped thinking about rules and restrictions, and our daughters left without a reminder of their curfew. This might seem a reckless omission at Costa del Sol, where nothing much happens before midnight, but Andrew and I refused to panic and get in a state. We took our time over a good meal, trusting the girls were safe and would do the right thing.

We were correct on both counts. Beatrice and Eugenie got back after we did, which made them feel wonderfully mature. But they'd also respected our standing curfew, and they were chuffed and proud about that, too.

A few weeks earlier, Beatrice and I had taken a different sort of journey together, this one to Russia. My daughter is a history buff, and she was thrilled to see the museums and the Kremlin. She was gripped by the story of her famous ancestors, Nicholas and Alexandra and Anastasia, and how and why the family was destroyed.

But while my children need to understand the monarchy and where they come from, I never want them to think that they are different or higher than others, because they are not. And so I took Beatrice with me one day on a tour of Hospital #3 in St. Petersburg, a place of long corridors and lonely cries, with too many children lying in rows of cots and too few nurses to attend them.

I would be criticized by those who deemed Beatrice unready for this experience. But I have a different view. I believe that teenagers can handle more than they're given credit for. They'll soon be taking charge of this world, after all, and they need to confront it sooner rather than later.

One of the most wrenching places in the children's ward was devoted to those with HIV-infected mothers. Most of these small patients had been abandoned here, some of them hours after birth. Before I knew it, Beatrice was holding a seven-month-old named Galina, quite unafraid to hug a child who was needy for contact. The baby promptly wet my daughter's new suede jacket, but Beatrice took it all in stride. (The nurse told her it was good luck—that she'd be back for Galina's wedding.)

Beatrice handled her first press exchange with aplomb. "I think we should definitely help," she told a reporter. "These children have to spend so much time here, and it's not the best place in the world. Something needs to be done." I was well pleased with her then, but even more so when she lagged behind me in the tuberculosis section and gave a five-year-old her hair-band, then bent to embrace her.

Toward the tour's end, a local television crew asked Beatrice her impressions. I marked it when she candidly answered, "It's such a contrast to what we see at home. I don't know what to say." In that moment she saw how selectively the world bestows its blessings. Our lesson was complete.

My daughter's jacket still has a stain on it, but she refuses to have it cleaned. It's a point of pride for her, and for a mother who trusted her to act her age.

LEARNING AND LIVING

*I*n December 1997, a week or so before Christmas, I was exhausted and run-down. I was showering on a Sunday evening when I felt a marble-sized lump under my right arm. In that moment the earth stood still. I saw my doctor, who recommended testing. By then I was deaf, and numb, because I was certain I had breast cancer.

Was I going to die? Would this be my last Christmas with my girls?

Due to the press of seasonal charity work, and perhaps some unconscious procrastination, I arrived on Tuesday for a needle biopsy at Lister Hospital in Chelsea, a center for cancer treatment. It would be three days more before I got the results. Three days when the orchestra of my mind blared out of control, the strings and brass in clashing time. Three days of lurking terror . . .

Until my doctor called with an all-clear: I had a benign

cyst. I cannot express how grateful I felt then, how humble, how *alive.*

My scrape with mortality was a powerful wakeup call. If *I* had been terrified while waiting on my tests, I could only imagine the plight of those in countries without such a strong medical system as ours. I vowed to get educated. I would find out that lumps in women my age, with no family history of breast cancer, were often harmless—though all of them should be checked, of course.

Belatedly, I saw that my enemy was simple ignorance. Had I been more informed, I might not have leapt to the most morbid scenario. I might have avoided those awful days of panic and paralysis. To help spare other women my experience, I now support a number of breast cancer organizations and try to raise awareness whenever the chance arises.

At the time of my scare, my father had a health concern of his own. In 1996, after his annual medical, a suspicious PSA count led to further testing, a diagnosis of early-stage prostate cancer, and a round of radiotherapy.

Dads is the Stiff Upper Lip personified, by training and temperament. At the start, he held his condition completely private. But in 1998, one of the newspapers called for confirmation that Dads was dying of prostate cancer. My father tried to dissuade them from printing anything at all. Failing that, he insisted that the story be accurate, and then he answered a few questions. When the article appeared the next day, he felt terribly violated. Whose affair was this but his, after all?

Two weeks later, another tabloid called and asked for an in-depth interview in return for a substantial charitable contribution. By then my father had learned a great deal about prostate cancer: that it verged on becoming the most lethal cancer for men; that it was no longer exclusively an "old man's disease"; that it often surfaced without symptoms; that a simple examination and blood test would tell the tale. He also knew, as he said, "how incredibly ignorant the average man is, worldwide, about the prostate."

Dads has always been an original man, one to go against the grain, and now he took an extraordinary step. He resolved not only to do the interview, but to become the nation's leading spokesman on the subject. At the start, some of his so-called friends called to ask why he was "washing his dirty laundry in public"—for a certain class in Britain, discretion is all. But Dads was undeterred. He has since undertaken a massive education campaign, with dozens of broadcasts and appearances all over the country.

At times he overdoes it and has to step back and rest a bit. But my father is determined that prostate cancer won't defeat him. He intends, as he says, "to carry on as long as I have the energy. We all have to get on with life, and in my way I'm getting on with mine."

By fighting back against his malady, by facing it head-on, Dads has found new pride and purpose. There can be no better therapy, I think, than the letters from men led by his example to get checked, and to an early detection that might have saved their lives.

Like me, my phenomenal father knows now that knowledge is our best ally—not only for our own peace of mind, but as a bridge to helping others act without fear.

SPENDING WISELY

Last summer I officially retired my seven-figure tax bill, got ahead of the game for the first time in memory. It was a proud moment, but I left the champagne on ice. In my experience, overspending is a lifelong addiction, not so different from compulsive gambling or a weakness for gin.

I am recovering but know better than to say I am cured.

In my twenties, I was the girl who'd thank her mother's boyfriend for a nice weekend with flowers—with some gargantuan bouquet that might have graced a Mafia funeral. If someone asked me to pick up cigarettes on a run to the shop, I'd return with five packs and refuse any payment, quite grand for a young lady who made a thousand dollars a month.

None of these acts was truly *generous,* in the strict and

selfless sense of the word. I hid behind my gifts because I suspected that no one would like me for myself.

Years later, as my marriage fell apart and life spun away from me, spending was my drug of choice. I'd buy things—a nice shirt, a pair of shoes, a trip to some exotic port of call—to keep from facing my depression. My credit cards had no limit, nor did I. At one point there were 450 people on my birthday gift list: family, friends, staff, friends of family, families of staff, etc.

My mantra never varied: *I'll pay the bill next month, and by then it will all sort out.* Which isn't so different from: *One more drink, and I'll stop tomorrow.* But tomorrow never came. My debt still weighed on my back, like some great feeding beast, until my days were an anxious blur. Sleep grew impossible. By 1995, when I had two daughters to house and no income to speak of, I was a breath away from going under. I could either go bankrupt or I could finally take control of my life. It was that simple, and that hard.

Perhaps I sensed that bankruptcy might be the end of me as a responsible person. Perhaps I feared the chaos would engulf me. I cannot say for certain what it was, but I decided to seize control.

It wasn't so complicated, really; I had to make more and spend less. Soon I was working seven days a week and actually applying it to my enormous bank debt. I stopped relying on my platoon of financial wizards and saviors. I made my own budget, which is to say I made a *plan*.

Three years later, the debt had been whittled away. I was on the road to recovery.

I understand far more about money now. I keep a close eye on my funds and my impulses. I still spend on the things that delight me, like my photography and my horse in Ireland, but I think before I sign the check. And if you get a present from me these days, it's more apt to be a picture I've taken than a sterling tray. I'll hope that you like the gift, and the giver as well, but I no longer confuse the two.

BREAKING PATTERNS

When I first visited Hale House, the Harlem facility for drug-addicted babies, I saw that it was lined with mirrors, all of them low to the ground. The best way to give children confidence, Mother Clara Hale explained, was "to say how beautiful they are when they look at their reflection."

I nodded my assent, but inside I was cringing. That very morning I'd caught Beatrice—then all of four years old—peering into a mirror at our hotel. "Don't be so vain," I told her. Even as I said it, I could hear Mum cutting me down when I was young, just as her mum had cut *her* down. I was upholding a family tradition and not liking it one bit.

That evening, after we got back to the hotel, I brushed my daughter's hair and said, "Aren't you a beautiful girl?" Then and there I decided I must start breaking patterns, for my own sake as well as my girls'.

First to go, as we've seen, was the Critic; next in line was the Judge. Through trial and error, I came to realize that nothing shuts off children faster than to sense they're in the dock. Instead of hearing evidence and passing sentence, or snapping my fingers to "solve" their problems, I've come to *listen* to my daughters and treat them with respect. As long as they are safe, after all, they are entitled to their own mistakes, their own lessons.

A candid relationship must cut both ways, which meant the Infallible Parent was also shown the door. Andrew and I have raised our children to be heard as well as seen. We give them strong boundaries without instilling fear in them—they have an original view of life, and why shouldn't they express themselves? At a recent lunch in the garden of the small house I'd just rented, the topic turned to where I should settle next.

"You should stay *here,* Mummy!" Eugenie said. "I love it here!"

"No," Beatrice decided, just as emphatically. "You should buy a home in America, because you'll be working there more now, and we'll be away at school." The two of them went on freely planning my life, leaving me to listen and marvel.

Next to be discarded was the Stiff Upper Lip. I was brought up to believe it was wrong to show emotions. If Mum told me off, I'd hide my hurt and agree with her, forcing a smile, just to keep the peace. But children are entitled to their feelings, and I've learned to let my daughters *live* their emotions, their anger and sadness as well as their elation. When they seem grumpy or snappish, I'll say, "Let's sit down and talk. Tell me, what is this really about?" I'll get them to open up, and soon I'll hear about some problem at school or a quarrel with a friend. Once acknowledged, the bad mood soon passes.

Nor do I swallow my own feelings in front of Beatrice and Eugenie. When my mother died, I left my door open and let them see me crying. I wasn't trying to be "strong" for them at a time when they'd lost their Granny. I was just *being*. They could see there is no shame in vulnerability, that it's part of the human condition we all share.

The last pattern to be broken, the one I'm still working on, is the Scapegoater. The other day I was in my bedroom, in dire need of some quiet time, when my daughters burst in to say good morning. "Not *now*," I said, with more teeth to my tone than I'd wanted. They later came round to apologize— they're wonderful girls, extraordinarily thoughtful—and I told them the fault was mine. I'd chided them out of my own stress and impatience; it had nothing to do with them.

They were just being children, after all, the one pattern I'd like to sustain as long as I can.

KEEPING FAITH

A few years—a lifetime—ago, I awoke to a uniquely despicable, libelous headline. If believed, it might have destroyed my family. I knew there was no shred of truth to it, but I had no money to sue.

I have never felt so helpless as I did that morning. I felt that I was strapped to the roof rack of my car, without an ounce of control over heading or speed, only the vain hope that I might hang on beyond the next curve in the road

In my *literal* car—the one I'd gotten into for no special reason, except that moving targets are less easily struck—I found myself by a church, off Marylebone High Street, and asked my driver to stop. I had never been to this place before, but I knew I needed help from a higher station.

I rang the bell and a young priest saw me into a tranquil reception room. I began to tell him of my distress, my terrible helplessness. "I don't know what to do," I kept repeating. "I don't know what to do."

And the young man said, "I may be a priest, but I also know a bit about life in the public eye." It turned out that his father was a prominent figure in British television. "You say that you don't know what to do," the priest went on. "But do you know the truth?"

"Yes," I said.

And the priest said, "Then hold onto it, because God knows the truth, and if you can feel it and really know it, then no one will ever get to you." I thanked him and left. I cannot say that the young priest righted my world, at least not there and then. But he restored to me a thread to hang on to: the thread of belief.

I think that I have always believed, going back to my girlhood with Grummy, a great supporter of the Church of England. But since that morning in Marylebone, my grip on my faith is so much stronger. Then I held on with my fingernails; now I enfold it with all my being.

Though I belong to no established religion, I revere many of them. I may choose to call my faith *God*; others may favor a different word. The label matters less than the conviction.

For me, faith means that what is right will win out one day. It means that the universe is not aimless but moves by some positive design. I can see this clearly now that I've stopped hiding—now that I've turned to *seeking,* instead. God is suddenly manifest to me. In reaching inside to discover who I am, I am also finding what I need.

Here is the new story of my life: I may have moved from the roof rack to the driver's seat, and it is good to be pointing the wheels for a change. But I also take great comfort in my sureness, at last, that I am not what makes the engine go.

TRUSTING OTHERS

*I*n *Adventures with the Duchess,* my special on ABC, one of my televised escapades led me to the crystal air of Colorado and to Montezuma's Tower. Known to climbers as a "cathedral spire," it is a jagged spine of red rock, 150 feet high.

The man in front of me, the one who would be blazing our trail and feeding me our single lead rope, was named Erik Weihenmayer. Though still quite young, he was a world-class rock climber. He was also completely blind, from a congenital condition that robbed his sight before he turned thirteen.

From the start, I was awed by Erik's knack for finding the smallest crevice with his fingertips, for knowing where to reach and how to stay out of harm's way. After he made it to the first narrow ledge, he called down, "Sarah, you can climb when you're ready!"

I am not a great one for heights. Had I taken Erik's invitation literally, our crew might have called our game on account of darkness. But there was no turning back. I reached with my arms and dug with my feet. At six feet off the ground, I was already in trouble. My fingers were sore and slipping; this was tougher than I'd thought. I became quite demanding: "Keep me tight on my rope!"

Halfway up, I had my first bout of vertigo. It brought the sinking feeling that I might not make it, that I might indeed fail. The climb grew even steeper. For a moment I lost traction, my feet scraping the rough rock. Just above me, Erik was clambering up the spire like a boy on a jungle gym.

At last I reached a decent platform, 25 feet from the summit. I looked up—at a sheer vertical wall, with Erik seated blithely on its top. "Listen, guys," I said, "I'm feeling really uncomfortable here." My breath turned shallow and raspy.

"Just relax," came a voice from behind me. "You're on a huge ledge." It was Jeff, Erik's business partner, the climber right behind me. He caught up and gave me an emergency backrub.

"You'll get totally anchored in," Erik shouted above the wind. "Don't worry!"

But I *did* worry—about the storm moving in from the

west, for one thing. The skies had darkened. The wind blew alarmingly. Would it sweep us off the face? Dizziness came over me in waves. For one awful moment, I felt so disoriented that I wanted to *jump off*, to do anything to get away.

Then I remembered what Erik had told me: *You don't decide when to climb the mountain; the mountain decides.*

My leader gave me my options. I could either join him at the top—and he believed that I could make it—or I could call it quits and back down. Here was my turning point. The blind mountaineer had my life in his hands. Could I trust him? Would I?

I took one tentative step up the wall. Then another. It was slow going, an agony, and I was terribly afraid, but gradually, strangely . . . *exhilarated*. Maybe I could do this!

Some interminable time later, I stopped again. I couldn't find my next handhold. "*Now* what do I do?" I said.

Erik smiled and said, "You just take in the view—you're at the top! What do you see?"

"The way down," I said, able to joke at last. Then I was reminded that this supremely competent person simply could not see. The balance had shifted; now Erik needed me. I clasped his hand and described the rugged landscape in as much detail as I could muster. He was returning my trust, and I did not want to fail him.

ASSUMING THE BEST

I'd come back into Heathrow after a frenetic round of business in the Midwest. My whole team was exhausted, and while waiting for my luggage, I let slip some remark about my own fatigue. It wasn't directed at anyone, really, certainly not at the baggage handler who took offense.

"Yeah, *right,*" the man retorted. "You don't know what work is."

This was back in the period when I almost dreaded coming home, because the only people in the United Kingdom who seemed pleased to see me were my children. Every slight would cue my sad Pavlovian response. I told the man, "Oh, please don't say that. You don't realize that I *do* have to work hard. *Please* don't believe what you read in the newspapers." And so on and so forth, in nauseating fashion. It wasn't enough that I'd put in a hard and honest week's work, and it had gone well, and I was proud of it. No, I couldn't be satisfied until this stranger became my friend—which meant, it's safe to say, that I wouldn't be satisfied in his lifetime.

I thought of the baggage handler more recently, when I went on one of the highest rated radio shows in Toronto. "Hello," the host began, pleasantly enough. "What do I call you?"

"Whatever you like," I said.

"Well, I think I'll call you Fergie, because that's a good name for a dog."

I thought, *Okay, this is a very nice start.* I had stepped back in time, to the days when I was fair game for any mouth with a mean streak. My host wanted the old Sarah, the one he could obliterate.

"So, Fergie," he went on, "what's it like using your royal title for commercial gain?"

That's a new one, I thought. At that point I probably should have hung up, but I sidestepped the question instead.

"Here's a good laugh," the man said. "Have you seen the outtakes of *Notting Hill* on DVD? No? Oh, you'll like this. Hugh Grant goes to his parents and says, 'Mummy, I've decided to marry a very famous redhead.' And the father throws up his hands in horror and says, 'Not that Fergie!

She'll take all your money and run away with another man!' "

Straining to stay cool, I said, "How very flattering that they should be using my name." I didn't know what else to say, but I somehow hung on the line till the interview concluded. I imagined all the good Canadians tuning in to my humiliation and chuckling along with the host. It took me hours to get back on my feet.

But then something remarkable happened. Listeners deluged the station's management with complaints about the host's behavior. By the next day my jovial assassin had acknowledged the fallout; he was just one rude man with a stale script, no less and no more. By standing strong and graceful under pressure, I'd brought others to stand behind me. By assuming the worst, I'd underestimated a great many people.

I tried to remember that lesson the next time I felt snubbed, at a polo match in Spain. It seemed that people were turning their backs and walking off away from me—not one or two, but a dozen or more. A few years earlier I'd have felt rejected, that people didn't like me because I'd messed up my life. I would have shriveled into myself and been sad for days.

But then I saw one passerby slip me a smile from afar, with a small wave. It wasn't personal, after all! Those people were shy and embarrassed and awkward, for whatever sundry reasons; they didn't know how to deal with me, and so they ran away. Or maybe some of them *didn't* like me, an opinion to which they were entitled. In either case, I would continue on my path and so would they, and it didn't much matter if we intersected or not. A turned back, I found, is sometimes just that—not an indictment, or even a dismissal, but a person simply going in a different direction.

Now that I see myself in a kinder light, I also glean more kindness from others—and imagine less cruelty. And when I do find myself under attack, I remember the saying: *The ones who care don't matter, and the ones who matter, don't care.*

SETTING FIRST THINGS FIRST

Like most working mothers, I spend more time away from my children than I like. I make it a point to have a proper parting with my girls, a lovely hug and some talk before I leave. So it went one recent Monday morning— except that I was in the car, and halfway to the airport through Windsor Park, when I realized that I'd forgotten to kiss Beatrice goodbye. She'd left earlier for school than Eugenie, and I was late and distracted, and then the moment was gone.

I slammed my feet on the back of the front seat, as if hitting the brakes, and cried, "We've got to go back!"

The driver tried to reason with me: "No, you've got to go on, or you'll miss your flight." On the other end, at a long table in a large room, a number of important businesspeople would be awaiting me.

I checked my watch and for a flash I hesitated, wondering what other plane I might snare to get me there in time. I am not oblivious to the needs of those involved in my career. In my prior lives, before Andrew, I worked as a publicist, an editor, a gallery assistant; I know the anxiety of counting on "the talent" to meet some obligation. I considered the consequences of a last-minute arrival and how it would place all of us under stress. I hate to upset anyone; I am deficient at playing the diva.

But ultimately I had a choice to make, and I put work in its place. "You don't understand," I told the driver. "I have to kiss my daughter good-bye." These days I'm prone to morbid thoughts like the rest of us—*What if something were to happen in the air, and I never saw her again?* But that's not what impelled me to go back—it was less dramatic than that. My career exists for my children. If I haven't seen my girls off right, I feel wrong the rest of the day. I'm unable to do my other job well if my *first* job lies undone.

We turned back to my daughter's school, a place where parents don't often pop up in the classrooms. I made my way down the hallway, a raging bull in a business suit and high heels, until I found the right room and rapped on the glass panel in the door. I caught Beatrice's eye and saw her face go all crooked in surprise.

She came out and said, "What are you doing here?" My

older daughter prizes our routines and gets taken aback when we depart from them.

And I said, "I just had to give you a hug, because I love you so much and I miss you already—you're my everything. I didn't say good-bye to you, and I'm sorry."

"But Mommy, you'll miss your flight."

"I don't care—there's nothing more important than you. That's the way it is, and I had to tell you that." And I hugged her, and then I had to go and run for it. I made the plane fifteen minutes before the door closed.

Another time it was Eugenie who had to be juggled. One day the headmaster's wife at her school stopped me and said, "You have to be with us at Eaton Theater on the twenty-sixth. We're raising money for Children in Crisis, and your daughter has a surprise for you. So you'll be there, won't you?"

This wasn't much notice, and I knew there was bound to be some conflict, but I also knew I'd have to work it out. "Of course I'll be there," I said.

When I got to checking my calendar, it came back to me. I'd been invited as guest of honor to a charity luncheon the day before the school performance. The day after the show, I needed to be in Manhattan—presumably bright-eyed and rested—for a business meeting. Both were ironclad commitments.

Neither was more important than Eugenie. So I worked it out. I hopped the redeye back to London Monday night, ran the girls to school on Tuesday morning, polished off some paperwork. Then I picked up my father and his family and drove out to a production of *That's Entertainment!* by St. George's Windsor School.

As the curtain rose, I had no inkling what lay in store. I had no idea that my daughter, age twelve, could sing like a dove—or that she had the lead role! Eugenie came in dancing, really *dancing,* swinging her hips to "Hello, Dolly!," belting out the song in a soulful contralto like some junior Shirley Bassey. With a superb boys' chorus behind her, she moved on to selections from *South Pacific* and *My Fair Lady.* She carried all of it off without a hitch, and by medley's end I was a flood of tears. My father was in tears. Beatrice—a clear bell of a soprano in her own right—was nearly jealous.

And Eugenie, my golden second daughter, was aglow. It meant the world to her that I'd traveled all the way back for her show. But how could I ever have missed that night? It is a memory I'll treasure forever. I'd gladly have circled the globe three times.

The next morning I flew back to New York. I was beyond jet lag. Still, I summoned my strength and sailed through the meeting. The work got done, as it always does, as I knew it would. If anything, I felt extra sure of myself and my bearings, because I'd known to put first things first.

SHELVING REGRET

When I went to interview the Dalai Lama in the Indian border town of Dharmsala, where he has lived in exile for four decades, I asked him what message he could have for his followers. Surely, I thought to myself, there must be terrible frustration after all these years—regret over missed chances, doubts about roads not taken.

But the Tibetan leader had a different outlook. The events of the last half-century, "both painful and otherwise, have passed," he said. "Time is always moving. The important thing is to learn from the past and then look forward to the future."

In the hours I was privileged to spend with this soft-spoken man, we talked of many things: of the future of his people; of spirituality and materialism; of world peace and individual responsibility. Toward the end, without my realizing it, he had turned the conversation back toward me. I found myself allowing that I still bore regret for mistakes I had made.

The Dalai Lama has the most remarkable dark eyes, sparkling and compassionate at the same time. Now they were trained upon me as he said, "Why do you live with regret? It's a waste of your energy. Regret is guilt, and there is no word for guilt in the Tibetan dictionary."

He was right, of course. At bottom, regret is a self-indulgence that helps no one. It is one thing to confess an error and make amends, quite another to wallow in mea culpas. By dwelling on past follies, we steal time and effort from the tasks ahead. We cheat the future. We vex all the friends who'd put our sins in the past if only we could do the same.

In my dark ages, when my name was a synonym for scandal, there were days so weighted with shame that I could hardly leave my bed, much less my house. I was the living dead. At my very depths, I reluctantly kept an engagement to speak before the annual conference of the Motor Neurone Disease Association, the first charity I'd adopted as my own. (In the U.S., the illness is known as Lou Gehrig's Disease, or ALS.)

When I got there, I felt so wretched and unworthy that I almost turned back at the door. Then I heard a familiar growl: "What do you think most people here would give to walk into that room?"

It was Kevin Langdon, a wry Australian who had willed himself to live with MND for more than a decade. Point taken. If Kevin could fight off his monstrous condition, telling jokes from flat on his back, how could I be consumed by my petty brush with infamy? It was time to get beyond myself and reconnect with the larger world.

Ten years later, I still wrestle with regret from time to time. But in my deepest heart I feel nothing to be sorry for, in the sense that I would live it all again if given the chance. There is no life without risk, no wisdom without misjudgments, no character without getting knocked down and picking yourself up again.

The good times and the bad have made me the woman I am today, and I have nothing to regret about that.

ESCAPING ROUTINE

For a number of years now, my daughters and I have spent the last two weeks of July in the Provençal hills, in a villa lent to us by my old friend, Paddy McNally.

Here is paradise, a setting that whets the senses. Fields of lavender and green olive trees stretch as far as I can see. Pine and eucalyptus and wild rosemary greet my nose, with a grace note of warm olive oil. Cobbled streets etch the near village of Seillans. Fountains mist the market square, in counterpoint to the still heat.

All is perfect harmony—and a jolt to your system, if you are coming from airports and meetings and reams of paperwork. The first few times I went there, I'd awake to the sultry air and the sound of crickets and the strange reality that my task was to relax.

Quite the tall order, as it turned out. The fast life is addictive, and I found myself craving the action I'd fled. I felt like a high-pressure cooker, like an engine that's revving when the car's locked in park. I tried to go early-to-bed, but my body had adjusted to its deficit of sleep. I grappled with insomnia, even with the aid of yoga and homeopathic drops.

It is only over the last year or two that I've begun to get the knack of vacationing. I remembered that "holiday" comes from "Holy Day," a time to pull down the shades and roll up the awning of one's internal shop. I took "vacation" back to its Latin root: *freedom, exemption, immunity.*

I went on strike.

Now I know to let *everything* go, especially for the first few days of decompression. To begin with, I keep no schedule. I get up in a very quiet way, and it may be eleven o'clock or three o'clock, since nobody bothers to wake me for lunch. My girls are well-trained in this. Now they're at the age when they like to sleep late, too, so it's a perfect arrangement.

When I decide to rise, I'll trot up to the pool and lie on my back. I'll read my book and have a bit to eat with a glass of wine, and I'll swim a few laps if I feel like it, or play a game with my daughters if we're in the mood. When the impulse strikes, I'll paint a watercolor or snap a photograph, or I'll point my bicycle to the nearest country lane.

I'll be done when I say so, which may be two hours later. Maybe I'll get to dinner at ten o'clock or maybe it will be ten-thirty, or maybe I won't have dinner at all. I'll go to sleep when I'm tired, whenever that may be. My routine is to have none.

My vacations work better this way, I've found. There are no sights I need to see except the purple hills and the faces of my girls. I am in a land where the magic rises with the honey sun, and all I need do is submit to it.

RESPECTING ELDERS

*I*t was a day not so different from a hundred others, yet I shall never forget it. Andrew and I had been booked together in northern England on ten royal engagements in the space of nine hours. As we proceeded from factories to schools, to a physical rehabilitation center, to a residence for people with Down Syndrome, I felt less and less adequate to the task. Everywhere I looked, there was such need and pain. I gave my all at each stop, yet what could I really do? How could my cameo make a difference to anyone?

It was early evening when we reached our final destination. I had a drumming headache, as much from sadness as fatigue. As our car rolled to a halt by a dull brick edifice, I made my way out and took a deep breath. We'd come to a home for the elderly. The residents would have been waiting all day for us, and I'd have to put my best foot forward. I wasn't sure I would make it through.

The walk was lined on both sides by spirited gray heads, waving their Union Jacks and calling out welcomes. We were nearly at the door when I passed a sweet-smiling woman who caught my eye. She sat in a wheelchair, and I could tell she'd had her hair done for us. She looked to be on the high side of eighty, and physically frail, but something I cannot describe drew me to her.

I did an about-face. I went up to her and said, "Hello, how are you? How long have you been waiting?" I looked into her blue eyes—and suddenly I got a massive surge of energy. It was the strangest thing; I no longer felt tired at all.

I asked the woman's name: Daisy. To make sure I got it, she sang a couplet from the old song: *Daisy, Daisy, give me your answer do . . .* We chatted on, and I soaked up the strength from that wise, lined face and those guileless eyes. I forgot that she was disabled. I took everything that woman could give me, and then I went into the home for our speeches and did the best job I'd done all day.

I met Daisy more than a decade past and never learned her last name, but I will never forget her. She brings to mind that wonderful scene in *Beauty and the Beast,* where the old man who comes to the door in rags is, in fact, God—

and if we ignore the light in his eyes, then what are we doing?

With age comes the long view of things. The elderly have weathered enough squalls to know that this one, too, shall pass. They own the courage to be original; they've learned to hold their own values above the conventional wisdom. Approached in the right light, they are neither burden nor drain. They are, in fact, a deep reservoir of strength.

At my lowest ebb in the mid-'90s, when I was the most reviled woman in England since Wallis Warfield Simpson, I received an invitation that stole my breath. It came from Robert Runcie, the Archbishop of Canterbury and head of the Church of England, who'd married Andrew and me in Westminster Abbey. He'd since retired but remained a strong pillar of the church establishment—and he'd be meeting me for lunch at his private club, where his closest associates would see us.

Whenever the world said I'd failed, Archbishop Runcie had defended me. Even after Andrew and I separated, he knew that we'd stayed true to the soul of our vows—we still honored and loved each other. In his evident pride to break bread with this redheaded pariah, he was taking his support one giant step further. The Archbishop cared nothing for what others thought of me. He discounted any gossip or a leak to the tabloids. He had too great a sense of perspective (and its cousin, a sense of humor) to give such trivia a thought.

Robert Runcie is gone these two years now, but I will long remember how he exercised the prerogative of age—to follow one's heart and instincts, and let the chips fall where they may.

SEEING THE LIGHT

I awoke to spring in New Orleans one morning, the light filtering through my lace curtain. The rest of the day would have to wait. I grabbed my camera to record the silent drama in my room.

Pictures drive me, you see.

Some years back, I worked with water colors, but brushes and canvases proved too cumbersome to pack, and I switched. Even so, everything for me is still a painting—a play of light and dark, a study in shadings. I compose my photographs the same way. An unapologetic auto-focus type, I am less interested in the mechanics than the vivid picture that seizes my eye and mind.

Photography is more than a hobby and less than a profession for me. I am an amateur in the root sense of the word; I am passionate about my pictures. My camera has led me to the light in the world and taught me to seek it in myself. At the same time, it reminds me that light is set off by shadow—that one defines and balances the other, like the sun and the moon. I think of my personal darkness, my setbacks and disappointments, and even my crises, and how they have impelled me to seek a brighter plane. In a sense, my pictures are emblems of my life.

Negativity is barred from my viewfinder. When I am *seeing* my subject, wholly focused, I cannot think of how the end product will be received. My critics (and even that worst one, my self-critic) fall quiet. This is the blessing of immersion, whether you are gardening or flying a helicopter. This is the gift of commitment, and I find it most easily these days through a lens.

I lack the discipline to keep a daily journal. In its place, I've compiled a pictorial diary of my life and travels ever since Beatrice was an infant, when Andrew was at sea and I became the family archivist. Now when I am far away and lonely, I take heart in my daughters' images. When ground down by work, I'm revived by a new batch of prints. Photography is my release, my consolation, my great adventure.

My avocation has allowed me to see what I might have missed. One day I was on the fourth floor of a modern hotel in Jacksonville, Florida, not your classic backdrop for visual glory. Suddenly the sunlight shifted and poured through a filigree of bridge cables. It was the light of revelation, of biblical epics. I clicked away, dazzled and excited to be there, anchored to the moment by the film I was exposing.

Of all my photographs, one carries special meaning for me: a mountaintop view of a vast, blue lake in Bariloche, Argentina. It was the last vista Mum and I took in together before she died. Whenever I look at it, I know there could be no truer "portrait" of my mother than this. It brings to me her inner core, the buoyant way she saw the world and made it sparkle through her eyes. That picture is a whole journal unto itself, a memoir in a frame, a touchstone for the visions we shared.

When I am able to capture such an image, I preserve an heirloom more valuable than any precious jewel: the history that knits our family now and for all time.

BENDING THE RULES

*L*ast summer, during our Spanish holiday, Andrew and I had forty-five people to dinner at one of the smarter golf clubs in Costa del Sol. They were all distinguished types, quite proper and much in awe of the Duke of York—and I treated them like crashers at a children's tea party. I purposely had no structured seating plan, no place names; I wanted to get more of a feel for our guests over drinks, then sort out in my head what would work. After dividing everyone into small groups, I guided them about like a toastmaster. "You stay there; you move to the left; shake a leg, you're over there; wait a minute, I don't know where you're sitting yet . . ." My guests huddled in their groups, laughing at this bossy redhead with her fractured protocol, and the ice broke all around.

Emily Post might have spun in her grave. But I was determined to give a proper dinner party *without* monotony, to make our guests comfortable yet surprise them as well. We were all relaxed and having fun—and isn't that the point of a social gathering?

Please do not take me wrong. I believe wholeheartedly in tradition. It is a culture's reference point, a well of standards and inspiration. I've written two books about Queen Victoria, whose courage and constancy move me to this day. But I also believe in adapting traditions to enliven us, not imprison us.

When I lived at Buckingham Palace, Sir Michael Timms, the assistant to the master of the household, taught me that history was more than a clutch of dusty dates. I learned, for example, that Andrew and I had waved from the same balcony that Prince Albert originally designed for Queen Victoria, as a grand stage to review her troops come home from the Crimean War. Soon I was giving my own tours, where I'd freely dramatize the chat between Albert and Victoria as to whether she really needed such a large balcony. I was never mocking or frivolous, but I added some romance and humor to the tale. I put my personal spin on it; I gave it an extra cutting edge.

When I started working for Wedgwood a few years back, I had the task of setting the table for Andrew's fortieth birthday party. With so many esteemed guests coming for dinner, I knew that our knives and forks had better be in the right place. I would have formal place settings, certainly, but with a twist. Instead of homogenizing the table, I mixed two different patterns—White Dolphin for the women and Seville for the men—with similar color schemes. In honor of Andrew's Royal Navy service, the canapés were set around models of ships and helicopters. On each table sailed a fleet of tiny wooden yachts. Once our guests saw the toys, they became easy and informal. Any awkwardness went out the window.

As a final departure from tradition, we showed a ten-minute video on the eventful life of Andrew and Sarah, including our wedding ceremony. I'm not sure of the reviews, but I can promise that no one was bored that night.

TAKING RISKS

I n 1998, I agreed to present a talk show for Sky Cable in Britain: a series of ten one hour programs on topics ranging from weight loss to murder. I was a seasoned television guest by then, but here, I'd be the host and interviewer, learning my craft and my subject matter as I went along. What's more, I'd be doing it on the British media's home turf, where I'd be shredded for the smallest miscue.

As the first taping date approached, I had huge doubts about my ability to carry a show. More than once I pondered pulling out. How could I find the courage to take such a chance? But something in me would not let go of the opportunity. I had a vague ambition to work in television, you see, and the intuition that this first try might open other doors.

So I went forward, on a wing and a prayer. I learned to do an auto cue and to time each segment of the show. Most critically of all, I learned to be myself on camera, which meant I had to trust that I was likable, a high hurdle for me. When my advisors asked me to list ten points I liked about myself, I was stymied at "one." Then they told me to list ten points I didn't like, and I ran out of paper.

Was this how Jay Leno started?

Wonder of wonders, the reviews were no worse than mixed. The TV critic at the *Evening Standard,* the top dog in the field, was actually positive. No one would have confused me with Oprah Winfrey, but neither did I fall on my face.

Some time later, early on in 2001, I received a call from Larry King. Of itself this was not unusual. Larry is my friend and mentor, and has taken me by the hand in all things related to television. But when he asked if I could stand in as host for him the following month, I thought he was joking. This was the big time, certainly out of my league.

Larry wasn't joking. I felt dizzy with euphoria and terror, especially after he said, "We'd love for you to interview Tiger Woods." I'd met Tiger when he was only twenty-one, at the Byron Nelson Golf Tournament in Dallas, a week after he'd won his first Masters by a historic twelve strokes. I walked the course with his mother, Tida, a tiny dynamo who moved so briskly that I got blisters keeping up. I will always be grateful for Tida's patience with a woman who scarcely knew a birdie from a sparrow.

Tiger and I became friends and stayed in touch, but I knew how busy he was, and that he mostly avoided interviews, and that he *never* did them in a studio. But when I asked him, it was easy. "For you, I'll do it," he said. I think he knew that I was serious about my work and how much the show meant to me.

This time the mountain would commute to Mohammed.

Once Tiger came on board, I was *really* terrified. I'd snagged an exclusive hour on national television with the most famous sportsman in the world, and I knew nothing about his sport and not a whole lot more about television. I sat down with Andrew (a six handicap) and Mark McCormack for background, but still I felt over my head. There is no live audience on Larry King, nothing to play off of—just the questions and the answers, and the questions had better be good. Whatever led me to believe I could do this? I confessed my nerves to Tiger before we went on: "Listen, I'm really worried that I'm going to dry up before the hour is filled. So just keep on talking, will you?"

Tiger promised he would and was true to his word. He handled the lighter questions deftly ("I'm an eight- to ten-handicap in fly fishing, but my buddy Mark O'Meara is a scratch") and was wonderfully earnest with the serious ones. He spoke thoughtfully about the racism his father encountered as a college ballplayer in the Midwest, about Nelson Mandela and Martin Luther King. He was charming and sincere about his passion for his game. By the second commercial, I began to enjoy the conversation for its own sake, almost forgetting the stakes.

The show ended too quickly, and I knew it was good. I felt deeply grateful to Tiger for his great gift of friendship, and to Sky Cable as well, even more so as I point toward my own syndicated show this coming year. I've seen how vital it is to take that first risk, that first step onto a new shore—for it makes possible the next step, and the next.

BINGEING NO MORE

*T*he craving struck on the road to Gatwick Airport, after I'd said good-bye to my girls for another ten days in America. Out of nowhere, I asked my driver to stop at a sandwich shop for a cheese-and-tomato roll.

"No, I won't," he said, in a surely-you-jest tone I found maddening. He knew what a slice of white bread meant to me, that there were biochemical implications here—that I was not so different from an alcoholic pleading for one short beer. "Why on earth," the man said, "would you want *that?*"

I insisted. Soon I was sharing the back seat with not one but two rolls, plus a monstrous Coke—half a gallon of the stuff, thick and sugary—to wash them down.

Let me explain about the cheese-and-tomato roll, a true British delicacy. It consists of cheddar cheese and tomato on white bread, with salted butter and mayo to bind it together. It contains a couple trillion calories, and I've never been able to eat just one. This was not, in short, what the doctor ordered for a woman who is under contract to weigh in once a month.

I stared at the rolls in their paper wrappings: a moment of truth. I reached for my cell phone, my lifeline, and rang Sarah Watson, my leader at Weight Watchers. "What's *wrong* with me?" I cried. "Why do I want to eat this?"

And she said, "Well, what are you unhappy about?"

I said, "No, I'm fine, I'm completely fine," but of course I wasn't.

Sarah said, "What are you doing right now?"

And I answered, quite spontaneously, "Leaving my girls." Sarah was wise enough to say nothing then, to let my words sink in. There was the problem in a nutshell. I felt miserably sad and guilty about leaving again, and I'd chosen cheddar and tomatoes over tears.

My bingeing dates back to adolescence, when Mum left our family for Argentina. I found consolation in sausages, several rounds a day, and in white toast "soldiers" and butter and boiled eggs, or Dads's signature weekend dish: scrambled eggs with cheese sauce. Later on, at our apartment in Buckingham Palace, I might squirrel away a chunk of Brie in our tiny refrigerator, to allay my pangs after the kitchen closed and I was alone again, with Andrew at sea.

In short, I knew all about comfort foods; I knew how to soothe my hurts with the aid of a plate piled high. I'd only forgotten that my old compulsions still ruled me, if I let them. I had to stay attuned to *what* I was hungry for, which may have nothing to do with an empty stomach.

That day I made a fair trade. I passed the rolls and cola to my driver—who downed them in a blink, the hypocrite!— and made another call. I told my girls how much I missed them and what a special time we'd have when I returned. Then I sat back to enjoy the ride, feeling utterly fed.

BREATHING DEEP

T wo summers ago I picked up a newspaper and saw a photograph of Geri Halliwell, formerly Ginger Spice, pretzeled into an extreme yoga position. With a spectacularly calm expression on her face, she seemed at peace with the whole wide world. When I'd recently met her, she'd exuded a similar serenity. *What is going on here?* I thought. *No one should be that calm.*

Rather than lose myself in envy, I opted to follow Geri's lead. I discovered that she was trained by a yoga lady named Katyana, and I rang up Katyana and asked if she could take a month off in August to teach me, too.

It was very tough at first. I had energy blocks from years of negativity, plus I was the sort of person who'd say she didn't have time to *breathe,* which is rather the point of yoga.

I was so stiff that I could barely bend over. It took a lot of work to break the walls and use my mind in a different way, but by the end of the month I was doing better. I was no longer so breathless. I was going at my own pace.

Now I get a huge benefit by simply breathing for five minutes. When you focus on the sound of your breath, and really listen to it, your naughty monkey-mind stops jumping from tree to tree. Your breath grows deeper and slower, like a warm breeze through long grass. Everything unclogs. You center on what's important, and the trivial falls away. You actually get more done out in the world—when you stop sprinting pell-mell, you see new trails of possibility.

And when life gets *really* stressful, I am like a bear in winter. I go inside myself. I walk more slowly; I use fewer words; I am economical in every way. I am taking a literal "breather" until I can get my energy back up.

I knew I was on the right track when I arrived in Orlando, Florida, after a week full of tension and taxes and other financial snarls. Before leaving the airport car park and plunging into my day, I borrowed the attendant's plastic chair (the poor fellow couldn't sit on it, anyway) and searched for a five-minute space. All I could find was a concrete wall, with a sliver of grass beyond it.

I sat there with my back to the wall, and closed my eyes and turned my head toward the sun, and slowed my heart and asked for strength. All about me were takeoffs and landings and bustle and congestion, but inside I was still. I stopped churning for solutions. And by the end of *that* week, it so happens, I found one—in no small measure, I'm convinced, because I allowed myself that one deep breath.

BEARING DIGNITY

The streets of Calcutta can be a whirl to the uninitiated: so much activity, so many people. When I was there, on a side trip after my visit to the Dalai Lama, it was hard to make sense of it all. Then I walked past an old woman sitting at a stall, and our eyes met. The teeming backdrop receded. We took stock of one another.

She was a seller of tea, and I can only imagine what kind of livelihood it provided her. Her mauve sari was threadbare, but she carried herself in a way that had little to do with poverty or despair.

"Good morning," I said. "You have such a lovely face. Could I have a photograph of you?"

Smiling, the woman held up her hand and said, "Hold on a minute." I could see that she had no idea who I was, aside from being European. She turned away from me and redraped her sari around her. When she wheeled back for the picture, I saw a small metamorphosis. It was as if the woman had gone inside herself and gathered all that was strong inside her. She'd been pretty before; now she was beautiful. It didn't matter that her sari was soiled or tattered. Her pride was a palpable thing.

"Cup of chai?" she said, when I'd finished shooting. She reached behind her and pulled out one of her handmade terra cotta pots, filled with steaming liquid. For an instant I wondered about the water and who might have used the small pot before me. But I could not possibly say no to her; I could not spoil her magnanimous gesture. I took the tea and thanked her and drank it down, then gave her back her pot.

"Oh, no," the woman said emphatically. "You are welcome in my country, and this is a present to you." I walked off a very humbled person. The tea seller had next to nothing, yet she'd pressed one of her possessions upon a person she had never met before and would never meet again. Had I ever seen such generosity?

Today that rough pot rests on my mantel, displayed like a piece of bone china. It reminds me that dignity resides in honest work and simple gifts, in the effort we take with a stranger, in our confidence to show our truest selves.

SAYING YES TO NO

My grandmother raised me on St. Francis of Assisi: *Seek to love, not to be loved; seek to understand, not to be understood.* I always thought it was wrong in God's eyes to say "no" —that you must always put others first. Besides, I wanted to be nice and to be liked and for everyone to think I was doing the right thing. For a budding people-pleaser, "yes" was so much easier.

My syndrome took full bloom in my Palace years. I did some very good things and some very bad, but in either case my life was driven by fear, not conviction. I set no boundaries or limits. People trespassed as they liked.

In September 2000, as we ran through the diary at my annual program meeting, I found a curious entry for October 15, my forty-first birthday. It seemed that I was scheduled to leave at seven in the morning to open an Austrian yogurt factory in the middle of England.

At first I thought it had to be a mistake. As my staff is well aware, my birthday is a sacred "no-go" day. I have a set routine: I get up and have breakfast with my girls and take them to school, and then we have a lovely birthday tea in the afternoon. How could I be on the job instead?

My then business manager, the one who'd set the day up, was proud as punch. "I've managed to do this for your charity," he said. The yogurt people would be giving Children in Crisis a handsome check, and my first thought was this: *I must think of the children.*

But my second thought was: *What about Beatrice and Eugenie?* I said, "I'm not going."

And my manager said, "I'm sorry, you've got to do it. I've agreed to it—I've made a verbal commitment."

I rang the yogurt executive to see if the date might be changed. He was a family man himself, he noted, and would love to accommodate me. But it was too late, he said. They'd printed the invitations, and the big boss was coming over from Austria. My business manager had waited several weeks before telling me, and now I felt boxed in. Though I hadn't signed a contract, I had the poor children in Silesia to think of, and the nice yogurt people, and my manager who'd given his word.

So I said what came easily to me; I said *yes.* I opened the yogurt factory and pleased just about everyone, and no one was let down except the two people I hate most to disappoint.

Flash forward two years to last summer, when I was being avidly pursued by a new management team out of California. (My former manager and I had parted company—as friends, I might add.) When I met Alan, the lead man, he more or less promised to take me to the moon. If I signed on the dotted line, he said, I'd become the biggest "brand" since Sinatra, or at least since Ovaltine.

When I pressed him for specifics, Alan would only say that I had to trust him. That seemed a lot to ask, since I didn't even *know* him. Alan became frustrated. I dug in. Finally, he blustered, "The trouble with you is you're too frightened to succeed!"

I didn't much like this treatment, but I'd been told that Alan was the *best,* a visionary of five-year plans, and I gave him another chance. Toward summer's end, he submitted a proposal to dictate every aspect of my life beyond the flavor of my tea, with a one-year fee that would stagger the economy of Luxembourg. A day or two later, he rang me at home. I nearly refused to take the call. I knew I could not tell him what he wanted to hear and that I'd be in for some bullying.

But I had reached my limit, and I did not defer that call or dodge it or delegate it. I took the phone. I calmly told Alan that I couldn't afford his services—and, for that matter, that I couldn't allow anyone to take charge of me.

He said, "Oh, you're just about fears and self-sabotage. You think I'm trying to control you!" His voice got quite loud. "I AM NOT TRYING TO CONTROL YOU!"

But I would not be bullied that day. I stood firm and trusted my judgment, and I thanked him and hung up. It was a historic moment, the first time I'd said *no* without a worry as to who might be upset. To mark the occasion, I wrote Alan a seven-line letter affirming my decision. As soon as I'd faxed it off, I felt a great weight lifted from me, because I knew I'd been true to myself. I saw that *no* can be as positive as *yes*—that it can define what you want in life by avoiding what you don't.

There is a coda to this story. Alan called me back the next week and apologized for his excessive zeal. He'd apparently learned a few boundaries himself. Since then we've had a more open relationship and may actually do a project together down the road.

But only if I feel like saying *yes*.

LIVING SMALL

*F*or a long time, when people asked me what I wanted of life, I was so swamped in confusion that I could give no decent answer. On the one hand, I had more material things than I'd dreamed of as a country girl. On the other, those *things* weighed me down, made me slow and sluggish. When my fairy tale soured, I worried obsessively that I'd lose them, which turned me timid and desperate at the same time.

Then one day it came to me: I wanted to get smaller. I'd been very lucky to live *big*—first at Buckingham Palace, then in my marital home at Sunninghill. There is a comfort in that sort of lifestyle, of course, and some vanity and ego attached to it, but I longed to downshift. I craved simplicity. I imagined a tidy house with no need for staff, a place I could run myself with the front-door key in my pocket.

My fantasy became real last winter. Ian Lowe, a man on my staff, found it on the Internet: a four-bedroom country house on an acre of land, forty-five minutes from London, near a sleepy village called Windlesham. I said, "What's it like?"

He said, "It's down a narrow lane, and you can sit outside in the evening, and it is perfect for you." I went out for a look, and found a white brick house with pine ceilings and a log fire and rooms of yellow and white. A sunny kitchen opened onto a sweet lawn and garden, where aspen and oak ringed blooming rhododendron.

The place was quiet and serene, oblivious to the roadway less than a mile off. It seemed almost . . . *compassionate*. Ian was right; it was perfect for me. I asked him to rent it straightaway.

Sunninghill, the house Andrew and I built, was a fine abode to us all, but I never felt truly at home there. Professionals did the decoration, and the sheer scale of the place dwarfed my prized possessions. Windlesham, by contrast, was a blank canvas. It stood ready for my brush, my palette. I brought back Mum's bits from Argentina, all the candlesticks and china and linens left her by Grummy, the silver cigarette boxes won by Hector at polo. I propped my little statues out in the garden. They stood there in gentle proportion, as though part of the original plan.

Once settled in, I found no greater pleasure than puttering around and opening my door to my guests. I felt private and unscrutinized, like a teenager whose parents had left for the weekend. My cozy rooms were ripe with possibility. I felt that *anything* might happen.

Six or eight years ago, I couldn't have stood the solitude. I wouldn't have known what to do with myself; I'd have wondered if something bad was lurking 'round the corner. But it's different for me now. I'm at ease in my own skin; I thrill to my new independence.

When the children went to the Queen's Golden Jubilee last June, I spent three of the most delicious days of my life alone here. A bank holiday weekend meant no work was brought around. I read and painted watercolors and watched the television, and stayed in bed when I wanted to. I made tea and scrambled eggs, and talked great sense to myself, and didn't have to be polite to anyone. I walked about my garden, the mistress of my domain. I knew every inch of it already, because the inches were relatively few

When the weekend was over, I felt proud to have been on my own, in my own intimate space—it was a first for me. After fifteen years of living under armed guard on too much ground, I felt a new sense of strength.

The lighter you travel, I think, the farther and higher you can go.

QUELLING PANIC

My childhood home was an old farmhouse where the floors would creak in the night. Someone was walking toward my bedroom, I'd be sure of it—not some ghost, but a real-life intruder! A baddy! I'd softly leave my bed, turn on my light, and pad into the corridor, where the noise was . . . and then I'd run the last, shadowy stretch into Dads's room, crying for help.

My father was a practical man, with no training in modern psychology. Had someone suggested that my panic in the dark bespoke a fear of dark things *inside* me, he would have been mystified. He had nothing to fall back on, save the sleepy parent's command: *This is ridiculous. Get back into bed!*

Twenty years or so later, my younger daughter came to me in the middle of one night. Pale and wide-eyed, Eugenie said, "There are dragons under my bed!"

And I said to her, "Okay, let's go and get the dragons away." I took a broomstick and shooed every last dragon from under her bed. Eugenie felt safe then, because her fears had been respected. Their power was broken.

I have my own dragons to this day. My claustrophobia turns elevators into hyperventilation chambers. I am also not so easy in the ocean, especially when it crashes over me. (Though I was married to a sailor, I much prefer terra firma.)

At the same time, however, I like to push myself to slay my dragons. In that spirit I resolved to dive in the Bahamas with Jean-Michel Cousteau, son of the legendary Jacques. Here was my ultimate nightmare: donning a heavy suit and sinking to the ocean floor.

To make it even more interesting, we layered on one more phobia, my quite reasonable fear of sharks. Jean-Michel assured me that we would be close enough to the toothy fellows to check their orthodontic work.

The plan was to go nine miles out, then forty-five feet straight down in forty pounds of chain mail. The suit was like Lancelot's armor, only with a Plexiglas mask and a device for underwater conversation. I felt like I was inside a sarcophagus, but I liked it when Jean-Michel drew a gutting knife across my torso and I could scarcely feel the tickle.

Looked at rationally and objectively, I was quite safe there on the sea floor. I had the latest gear and the perfect guide; I was absolutely protected. But my rational mind went elsewhere when the first flotilla of Caribbean reef sharks came gliding overhead. I felt like I was standing on a runway at O'Hare with six planes bearing down at me at once.

Sharks like to nudge you, to get a feel for what you might taste like. The first time it happened I must have let out a yelp in my mask. Jean-Michel said, "See how gentle and elegant and perfectly streamlined they are." *And, oh, what big teeth they have . . .*

My heart in my mouth, I reached up to stroke a white belly, as smooth as satin. Up close, the six-foot shark looked like an overgrown rubber bath toy, and gradually I relaxed. The sharks were beautiful, really. They bore me no malice. They did get excited when we held up spears with chunks of fish, a sort of shish kebab in the raw. But while they snapped at their hors d'oeuvres and at each other, the sharks showed little interest in making me their main course.

When the snacks were gone and our air ran low, I returned with Jean-Michel to the surface. I felt nearly weightless with achievement; I had shooed away my worst fears.

My next elevator did not stand a chance.

GOING ONE ON ONE

My girls are lovely together. Sibling rivalry is nevertheless a fact of life, and it does us all good to break away from it, whether on an outing to the mall or a trip to a special place. At some point during the summer, I try to take three or four days alone with each of my daughters, to give them my undivided attention. We find a special cadence and closeness on these private excursions; we have some of our very best, most intimate talks.

On one such occasion, with Beatrice already back to school, Eugenie and I chased the last rays of summer in Nassau, the Bahamas. We found a man with a seaplane and reasonable charter rates, and made a plan one morning to go to Harbor Island to visit friends. As we flew on, however, I could see some dark clouds thickening over our destination.

I said to Eugenie, "What else are we doing today?"

She confirmed that we had no pressing event.

"Then what would you say about changing course?" As itineraries are more easily set (and reset) with one child than two, we soon reached accord. Addressing our pilot, I said, "Marcus, turn left here, please." There was lovely weather to our south, and why shouldn't we follow the sun? It was simple enough to call our friends and let them know we'd be there in time for tea.

We flew south for forty minutes, when Marcus had an idea. Pointing to the pristine sand of Exuma Island, a place I'd never heard of, he said, "A friend of mine has a restaurant on that beach. Why don't we land the plane and have lunch?"

My daughter and I agreed that this was a brilliant improvisation, and our faith was rewarded. No sooner had we deplaned than we met a snowy gull—"I think I'll call him Eric," Eugenie said. With her new friend waddling along the sand behind her, my daughter found a perfect conch, which I still have with me now. We walked a bit farther, holding hands, till we came to a small wooden shack, simple and clean, with a menu that was swimming that morning. Though Eugenie is a confirmed carnivore, she loved the grilled fish there because it was so fresh.

When our plates held but shiny bones, we retraced our steps over the white sand. We boarded the plane and swung back to Harbor Island, which was sunny again. I think that Eugenie will long cherish that day, when she had me—and Eric, and our impromptu lunch—all to herself.

SLOWING DOWN

On one typical morning, I ran Eugenie to school and rushed back to Sunninghill on a shortcut through the park. I knew I had a busy day ahead: first an interview on my photography, then a charity lunch, then Eugenie's netball match. It was one of those days, as the saying goes, when I was going so fast that I'd be catching myself on the way back. *I have to hurry,* I kept thinking.

Pushing the speed limit, my nerves jangling, I had blinders on to the green splendor around me. Had you quizzed me, I could not have told you a single thing about the park that day—until I caught a glimpse of some pheasants to the side of the road.

Then I did what I sometimes do when I've been whooshing through life till I'm lost in my own momentum. I gave myself permission to *stop.* I pulled over and took a big, deep breath, and I got out and walked around my car three times . . . slowly. I said to myself, *Why am I in such a rush? Why can't I calm down and watch and look?*

I crept up to the pheasants. There were three of them, two cocks and a hen, and I realized how amazing it was to really *look* at these exquisite birds. I studied the males' red faces and wattles, the "eyes" in their tails, the iridescent collage of their feathers. How did a creature so extraordinary come to evolve that way? How exactly did that happen? I sat there for a good ten minutes, and when I left, I felt ten times as alive as when I'd stopped.

Once you become more conscious of the world around you, amazing things begin to happen. I can sit fascinated by the colors of an apple, by how the red flows into the green. Or by the pores of a strawberry, or the veins of a flower. Not long after my pheasant encounter, I was driving to dinner with friends through Grosvenor Square, a busy London intersection near Hyde Park. As we approached the crossroads, I suddenly saw a fox, of all things. He stood frozen atop a wall that bordered the walk, not twenty yards from our car. As we pulled to the curb and cut our lights, Mr. Fox saw it was safe and hopped down onto the walk.

A homeopathic doctor in India once put this to me metaphorically: "You are on a rickety bus from Bangalore to Bombay. My bus may be very old, and it may not be very fast, but it will make it to Bombay one day. And so why do you run up and down the bus to make it go faster? Is it not better to sit and enjoy the trip?"

I looked back to the wall, and then I saw Mrs. Fox, clearly pregnant, waiting for her mate to bring home the bacon—in this case, from an open rubbish bin that had fallen off the back of a cart. Mr. Fox made three trips to the bin and back, and my friends and I sat for minutes and watched the whole Disney spectacle of it. Even in a great city, where we've done our best to dam nature up, to hurtle by without intrusion, it can pop out at you at any time. But you have to do your part; you have to decelerate your racing mind to notice. I have taken to bicycling of late and have seen whole worlds that are invisible from a rushing car.

There is a sign on a country road that always makes me laugh when I pass: SLOW DOWN; FROGS CROSSING. It might seem a joke, but I believe there is great wisdom in that sign. It prods me to acknowledge the life around me, however seemingly inconsequential. To mesh one's tempo to the rhythms of nature. To pause every so often to raise your head, so you can see down the road you've taken, and where it might be leading you, and the unexpected pleasures it may bring along the way.

COMING HOME

On September 10, 2001, one day before the world changed, I arrived in New York to receive a "Mothers and Shakers" Award from *Redbook*. As I took my seat, I felt unprepared. I hadn't known it would be such a big affair. I worried that I didn't have my speech right.

Looking back at it, my discomfort came from something more essential: I missed Mum. At other tables, I saw the honorees sitting next to their mothers, sharing the great moment. But I had no one there from whom to draw support. My mother had died three years earlier, and it seemed like a fortnight—and an eternity.

That afternoon shook me to my core. I thought I had acknowledged the death, and surely I had *felt* it. When I met my sister, Jane, in Buenos Aires to take care of Mum's affairs, we were stunned to see the mean one-bedroom apartment where she'd recently moved after losing her ranch to debt. She must have carried a terrible weight, yet she never complained. She remained the most energetic, optimistic, unselfish woman I knew, with loads of presents for her grandchildren at every visit.

But I hadn't really begun to grieve for Mum, not with my heart and soul, until the day of my *Redbook* award. Now I was consumed by the hole in my life. Everywhere I looked, in stores and restaurants and coffee shops, I saw mothers and daughters having a day out together. It was all so mundane and unremarkable, and yet there were needles in my chest. I missed the sense of being so very special to someone. I missed the one who *knew* me longer than any other.

I was still feeling incomplete last summer, when I took my daughters to southern Spain to present the Susan Barrantes Trophy for polo. I went reluctantly, with a sense of foreboding. Since Mum's death, I had not been overeager to see her old haunts and old friends. I knew the void she left would be inescapable in Spain, like a black hole with terrible gravity.

Everyone who'd loved Mum was there, of course, all the people I'd known from polo circles from before my teens. I saw the Domecqs, of sherry fame, and many others whose names I'd lost through our thirty-year hiatus. They were all so pleased to see me, so warm and affectionate, that I couldn't stop smiling.

Señorita, how are you?

Do you remember me? Do you remember how you held my sticks? Here was Ignacio Domecq, my first crush, now married with five children. When I was twelve, and Ignacio a year or two older, he came to stay with us to learn English and play polo. He had his eye on my sister, Jane, but I was mad about him, anyway. Mum took him on a tourist outing one day to Blenheim Palace, with me next to him in the back seat. I allowed a bump in the road to jar my hand to Ignacio's knee—such bliss!

Here were the dashing Argentines, the men I remembered from when I was seventeen and went to visit Mum and Hector, when I galloped with the gauchos against the unbroken sky. Robert James, Hector's best and oldest friend, squeezed me in a bear hug. I was suddenly back in the old life I once knew with Mum, with its musical language and old-fashioned ways, when I had no reputation and could simply be myself.

In my speech, I told my friends—for I saw they *were* my friends, too, and always had been—how grateful I was for their coming. I said, "I'm very pleased that my girls are here. I was the same age when I first met the Domecq family—" I was about to say that I wished Mum were still with us, but I missed her so much in that moment that I could not continue.

I sat down to lunch next to little Hector, a darling ten-year-old who was Mum's godson. When he seemed sad and I asked him why, he said, "Because I loved your mum so much." Then he showed me his secret box with pictures of my mother, and I held his face and said, "Hector, I could never replace my mum, but could I be your god-mother?" He looked at his mother and then away, before shyly nodding his assent.

Later Hector's mother revealed to me that he had asked the month before if Susie had any daughters, and if one of them might ever become his godmother. As she told me this story, it was like a summer sun breaking through a dense sky. My sadness lifted. I felt almost whole again. In that sunny Latin land, in a region I'd never been before, I had somehow come home.

FINDING REFUGE

*E*ight years ago, I had a chair made especially for us, a fat green canvas armchair. It is casual and unpretentious, and roomy enough to plant a daughter on either side of me. It's in its third house now; wherever we go, it goes.

When I first brought the chair home, and my life was still a muddle, I'd take to it after putting my young girls to sleep. There in my bedroom, surrounded by pictures and mementos, I'd close my eyes and pretend that I was Dorothy from *The Wizard of Oz*. I was outside that little house in Kansas and the whirlwind was coming, and Toto and I would be blown to bits if I didn't chain us fast to the gatepost. . . . That whirlwind was my restless mind. Every time it went roaring off to some mundane issue, great or small (*Have I done the flowers for dinner? Have I checked the girls' homework?*), I brought myself back to the gatepost—my chair—and held on for dear life.

My life is less stormy now, but I still need a safe zone where no one can get at me. The chair soon triggers a heavenly, floating state. I might pray for a while, or simply think upon my blessings. I have no worries; I am utterly at peace. (When I'm away from home, I can find the green chair in my mind to similar effect.)

My girls and I still share the chair on weekends whenever we can. The arms have worn a trifle thin, and the springs are sprung, so we sink deliciously into the seat—it's better than new. We watch Cary Grant and James Stewart and Ingrid Bergman, from an era when good talk mattered more than special effects, and we're lost in the film and our company. We've been through a lot of change in the past eight years, Beatrice and Eugenie and me, but our chair is a point of continuity. It declares that wherever our separate journeys take us, we will always be together, that our love and closeness will endure.

TAKING NO ONE FOR GRANTED

*E*ight years ago I hired a gentle young man named John O'Sullivan as my personal assistant, based in New York. He won me over with his calm intelligence, but I had yet no idea of the gem I had found. Johnny would become one of my best friends and most trusted advisors, my brother and protector. He speaks three languages; his political briefings would be worthy of the State Department. Still, he remains as humble as the day I met him.

Early on September 11, 2001, Johnny escorted me to the *Good Morning America* studio in midtown Manhattan. At approximately 8:40, I finished my interview and returned to the green room for my briefcase. Finding Johnny glued to a monitor, I said, "What's going on? We've got to go."

"An airplane has just gone into our office," Johnny said.

My American charity, Chances for Children, was based on the 101st floor of the north tower of the World Trade Center, in a space donated by my great friend Howard Lutnick and his firm, Cantor Fitzgerald.

There must be some mistake, I thought. *This cannot be happening.* I stared up at the screen, at the charred hole where great clouds of black smoke were now billowing—at the spot where Johnny himself might have been, had my calendar put me at home that day instead of working in America.

Johnny's face was white. He frantically called Kenneth Merlo, our charity's managing director, who came to the office by 8:00 each morning, like clockwork, after dropping his daughter at school. I cannot remember the last time Johnny raised his voice, but when he got through on Ken's cell phone he was screaming, *"Where are you?"*

Sounding puzzled, Ken told him, "I'm at Sharon's house." He was running late that day because he'd stopped off to help one of our consultants with a computer glitch. Immersed in his task on the Upper East Side, he was unaware of the tragedy unfolding a few short miles away.

Though we now knew that our small office was empty, my dread stayed at a full gallop. By the end of that cataclysmic day, I'd learn that Howard had been spared by mere chance, much like Ken. But more than 700 others at the firm were lost, many of them known to me, including Howard's younger brother, Gary, and a rare spirit named Samantha Egan, age twenty-four.

We'd borrowed Samantha from Cantor Fitzgerald the year before, to help with some administrative tasks, and soon she was running Chances for Children on her own. Nearly six feet tall, with a quick smile and a cheery voice, she lit up any room she entered. Above all, Sam was *unconditional*—in her energy, her passion, her commitment to helping children. When she wasn't working or Roller Blading, she was studying for a degree in education. Naturally kind, game for anything, she was meant to be around the young.

Even after passing the reins to Ken last May and moving back down the hall, Sam would volunteer to do something for us every day. I am afraid we might have taken her loveliness for granted; we assumed she'd always be there for us. She was that constant, that true.

Chances for Children kept on, as we all must. We found temporary space with the help of John Mack at Credit Suisse First Boston, then an office donated by Bloomberg LP. But none of us will ever be quite the same. Whenever I think of September 11, I see Samantha's sweet face, and I thank God that Johnny was spared, and I wonder at the thin line between life and the grave. When tragedy strikes, be it in war or natural disaster, we are awed and appalled by the numbers lost. We are *touched* by the one life we knew, that single person who has no less value than the mass, the spirited woman who loved to Roller Blade and dance.

From Samantha Egan I learned that tomorrow is promised to none of us, not even the young and pure of heart.

LIVING ON

Among the people I hold dear, death has a bitter habit of calling before its time. When my stepfather died so prematurely, and then my mother, and Diana, I was destroyed each time. I could find no logic in their dying, no acceptance. I found only pain and loneliness.

Then, three autumns ago, I lost Carolyn Cotterell. She was forty-three years old, with three young children. She was my best friend, my guardian angel, the greatest teacher in my life.

We went back nearly twenty years, to when we were young and single and striving to make our way in London. Carolyn Beckwith-Smith rented me a room out of her apartment for $50 a week. All I owned was a narrow bed and a chest of drawers, but I also had Carolyn, the perfect roommate. She took me under her wing when I was a mass

of insecurities; she listened patiently to my weight problems and make-up problems and boyfriend problems, and
gave her gentle counsel when asked.

Carolyn was the soul of generosity, except for the night
that I plundered a lonely chicken leg from our refrigerator.
I hadn't known that this was Carolyn's big night—that
she'd graduated to a bit of poultry after weeks of a strict
fruit-and-black-coffee regimen. (We were always dieting,
except when we were bingeing.) When she discovered the
drumstick was gone, only her deep moral values kept her
from strangling me on the spot.

When the tabloids discovered that I was seeing Andrew, and platoons of photographers dogged my every step,
Carolyn would hide me in the trunk of her car and take me
where I needed to go. She wasn't above a sly prank in a
good cause.

Later on, after I'd worn out my welcome in Buckingham
Palace, she would say to me, "Fergatross, just remember
this. You walked into the Royal Family in blue jeans and
you can walk out in blue jeans. You have yourself, and you
don't need anything more."

I had relied on Carolyn my whole adult life, yet she
never seemed to find me a burden. She gladly became god-
mother to Beatrice. She was a strong and spiritual Catholic
who gave from her very core, and she gave to me without

chalking a ledger. There were times we would meet and not say a word. We'd look into each other's eyes and start to cry, out of the simple joy of seeing one another.

The end began with a freckle, a tiny mole on her foot. With violent speed, the mole became a melanoma running up her leg and beyond. There were crushing treatments and moments of hope, but the cancer would run its course.

I last saw Carolyn at her friends' house in Los Angeles, between rounds of chemotherapy. I had twenty minutes between planes; she had the stamina for barely that long. I asked her how she was standing the pain. She told me that when she lay awake at night, she would look at her little Blessed Lady, kept near her bed, "and it gives me the strength to know that I'm not on my own."

But Carolyn was not one to dwell on the darkness. "Remember the blue jeans, Fergatross?" she said, finding a smile through her pain. "We'll both walk through the woods again in our blue jeans, won't we?" Then she turned pensive: "Do you think I'll ever get to see Poppy get married?" A dear and thoughtful eleven-year-old, Poppy was Carolyn's eldest child and my goddaughter.

I said, "Of course you'll see her get married. You *have* to be there." I was trying to will her to live.

As I made to go, Carolyn said, "Please take my Blessed Lady with you."

"I can't do that," I said.

And Carolyn, with typical foresight, said, "You'll need it more than I will."

When she died, not long thereafter, I could not see how I could live without her. I felt numb. Inconsolable. The world dimmed and flattened in my sight. For weeks I went through the motions of living, unsure of its point.

I was in bed in my hotel room one night, fighting sleep. I happened to glance at the Blessed Lady, which I keep with me wherever I go. I felt suffused with an old warmth—the feeling of *Carolyn,* who gave to the end.

I had lost the physical person, but the feeling—the essential part of her—endured. I'd mislaid my friend in the tangles of my grief, but she had never really left me. I still held her words and wisdom in my head, her selfless love in my heart.

She will live on inside me as long as I draw breath.

LOVING WELL

Andrew and I were in our midtwenties when we courted and married, not children by any stretch. But did we really understand what we were doing? My bridegroom had lived a fairly sheltered life, from Palace to school to Royal Navy to marriage, within tight confines at every step. I'd probably had more exposure to the world—I'd traveled and worked and kept an apartment—but emotionally I was even more naïve than he.

After circumstances (and a matchmaker named Diana) threw us together, we had a wonderful time. Andrew was gentle, steadfast, bright, and full of fun; I would do anything to please him. We were children in a candy store, doing as we liked, never thinking of tomorrow. When my husband was shipped off to sea 320 days a year, our marriage was bound to sink, and it did. Painfully, regretfully, we released each other to the world, where our adult lives began.

We still feel pain and sadness for that parting, but regret now lies behind us. Had we not gone our separate ways, we could never have learned what we needed to get to where we are now. We could never have understood ourselves, much less each other. By divorcing, we laid the foundation for our successes to come—as friends and parents and maturing adults.

It was a hard-learned lesson, perhaps the hardest of my life, but I value it well.

Unity is born of mutual strength, not weakness; Andrew and I are strong enough at last to stand in iron solidarity. We live in trust and respect and total honesty. We know the worst of each other and the best. We have nothing to fear or hide.

On the day of our separation, more than a decade ago, we took our respective lawyers to dinner—at a single table for four. From the start, then, we flouted the "rules" for divorce. We made up our own to honor our living history together—that we were once very much in love, in the landmark relationship of our lives. And that we loved each other still.

I know that people find our arrangement curious. They wonder how we sustained such a close bond once our "official" tie expired. My short answer is this: We know who we were *then,* in the flush of our young romance, and we know who we are today.

Six years ago, when I could no longer afford the upkeep on a rented house, Andrew invited me to live in our family home. There was never a question between us, just a natural extension of the most profound friendship that either one of us has ever known. Sunninghill was quite spacious, after all. I would live downstairs and Andrew up, and the girls would get to see more of both their parents. It seemed to us a win-win-win-win situation.

And so it was, until recently, when I spread my wings again and found my own abode. Our addresses notwithstanding, Andrew and I remain as close as ever. We tend our relationship much as any two people who care about one another, be they friends or spouses or somewhere in between. We forgive and forget; we apologize after an argument, even when we think we're right; we refuse to end the day angry.

We have a near-perfect relationship, in fact, which leads to the second question I face rather frequently: Why don't we reconcile?

To that I offer one more simple answer. Andrew and I will not remarry precisely because we *like* where we are now. Our relationship suits us as it is—why squeeze it into a compartment or someone else's fairy tale? Why can't our fairy tale end like this: *And they both lived happily ever after, the most fantastic friends the world has ever known.*

The marriage was the marriage, and that is over. But ours is the wedding of the souls, and we've never parted, and never shall.

AUTHOR'S NOTE

This book would not have been possible without one person and his belief in me against all odds.

In 1996, Sir Anthony O'Reilly, the chairman and chief executive of HJ Heinz Company, offered me a job as representative for Weight Watchers. It was at a time when my public persona and self-esteem were at their lowest, and my first reaction was disbelief. How could this extraordinarily successful businessman think that I could undertake such a huge role? How could I possibly promote a global company with 675,000 members in the United States alone? How could I address meetings of thousands of people who would look to me for inspiration and advice?

Racked with doubt, I told Tony of my fears and inadequacies. But the man was not to be dissuaded. He knew that due to my celebrity, I would be in a position to promote an organization and its philosophy on weight and health. To this day, I marvel at Tony's trust and belief in me. His outstretched hand of friendship came at a pivotal point in my life; he returned me to the land of the living and thus gave my children their Mommy back—a Mom who had been lost in the wilderness. Now I had a positive focus for my energies and a path toward independence. Even better, my job would take me the length and breadth of a country I was growing to love.

Without that job, and that friendship, I dare not think what might have become of me.

As I have learned, once you gather the courage to make a first tentative step toward your goal, the next ones come easier. My work with Weight Watchers has led to a job as a spokesperson for another O'Reilly company, Wedgwood China. They make a product that is dear to me, as it represents all that is quintessentially British.

Belief, trust, conviction—they are powerful lessons to all, and I have found no one better to teach them than Sir Anthony O'Reilly.

AUTHOR'S NOTE

*T*his book would not have been possible without one person and his belief in me against all odds.

In 1996, Sir Anthony O'Reilly, the chairman and chief executive of HJ Heinz Company, offered me a job as representative for Weight Watchers. It was at a time when my public persona and self-esteem were at their lowest, and my first reaction was disbelief. How could this extraordinarily successful businessman think that I could undertake such a huge role? How could I possibly promote a global company with 675,000 members in the United States alone? How could I address meetings of thousands of people who would look to me for inspiration and advice?

Racked with doubt, I told Tony of my fears and inadequacies. But the man was not to be dissuaded. He knew that due to my celebrity, I would be in a position to promote an organization and its philosophy on weight and health. To this day, I marvel at Tony's trust and belief in me. His outstretched hand of friendship came at a pivotal point in my life; he returned me to the land of the living and thus gave my children their Mommy back—a Mom who had been lost in the wilderness. Now I had a positive focus for my energies and a path toward independence. Even better, my job would take me the length and breadth of a country I was growing to love.

Without that job, and that friendship, I dare not think what might have become of me.

As I have learned, once you gather the courage to make a first tentative step toward your goal, the next ones come easier. My work with Weight Watchers has led to a job as a spokesperson for another O'Reilly company, Wedgwood China. They make a product that is dear to me, as it represents all that is quintessentially British.

Belief, trust, conviction—they are powerful lessons to all, and I have found no one better to teach them than Sir Anthony O'Reilly.